A Practical Guide to Action Research and Teacher Enquiry

This accessible guide will be an invaluable resource for early years practitioners looking to make a positive difference in their settings by using action research or teacher enquiry. Guiding readers through the practical steps, issues, and potentials of conducting research in a variety of early childhood settings, the book will increase practitioners' confidence, enabling them to bridge the gap between recognising room for improvements and instigating necessary changes.

Divided into easy-to-follow sections, *A Practical Guide to Action Research and Teacher Enquiry: Making a Difference in the Early Years* offers clear definitions and explanations of action research along with explanations of how it can be applied in early years settings to effectively and efficiently improve outcomes for children. Chapters outline a clear rationale for engaging in action research, highlight purposes and potentials of various approaches, and provide a helpful step-by-step discussion of the different stages of enquiry. Ten examples of practice are used to clearly illustrate the action research cycle in a variety of settings, and in relation to a range of topics and ages, thereby providing readers with a wealth of tried-and-tested ideas for application in their own settings and projects. These are supported by a range of downloadable resources which can be used as tools to support the planning, reflecting, and evaluation of practitioners' research activities.

Informative, inspiring, and highly relevant to practice, *A Practical Guide to Action Research and Teacher Enquiry* will support and scaffold the research activities of early years practitioners, managers, and students.

Amanda Ince is Programme Leader for the MA in Early Years Education and the MA in Primary Education programmes at the UCL Institute of Education, UK.

Eleanor Kitto is Programme Leader for the Early Years Initial Teacher Training programme at the UCL Institute of Education, UK.

A Practical Guide to Action Research and Teacher Enquiry

Making a Difference in the Early Years

Amanda Ince and Eleanor Kitto

Routledge
Taylor & Francis Group

LONDON AND NEW YORK

First published 2020
by Routledge
2 Park Square, Milton Park, Abingdon, Oxon OX14 4RN

and by Routledge
52 Vanderbilt Avenue, New York, NY 10017

Routledge is an imprint of the Taylor & Francis Group, an informa business

British Library Cataloguing-in-Publication Data
A catalogue record for this book is available from the British Library

Library of Congress Cataloging-in-Publication Data
Names: Ince, Amanda, author. | Kitto, Eleanor, author.
Title: A practical guide to action research and teacher enquiry: making a
difference in the early years/Amanda Ince and Eleanor Kitto.
Description: Abingdon, Oxon; New York, NY: Routledge, 2019. | Includes
bibliographical references and index.
Identifiers: LCCN 2018050783 (print) | LCCN 2019005890 (ebook) |
ISBN 9781351024587 (eb) | ISBN 9781138495166 (hb: alk. paper) |
ISBN 9781138495180 (pb: alk. paper) | ISBN 9781351024587 (ebk)
Subjects: LCSH: Action research in education. | Inquiry-based learning. |
Teachers–Training of. | Education–Research–Methodology.
Classification: LCC LB1028.24 (ebook) | LCC LB1028.24 .I53 2019 (print) |
DDC 370.72–dc23
LC record available at https://lccn.loc.gov/2018050783

ISBN: 978-1-138-49516-6 (hbk)
ISBN: 978-1-138-49518-0 (pbk)
ISBN: 978-1-351-02458-7 (ebk)

Typeset in Melior
by Cenveo® Publisher Services

Visit the eResources: www.routledge.com/9781138495180

Contents

Acknowledgements

Thank you to all of the amazing early years practitioners whom we have been fortunate to work with. In particular, we would like to acknowledge the contributions of the following individuals and organisations who have been so generous in sharing their projects, insights, and reflections for the purposes of this text.

Aberdeen Park Nursery
Blean Primary School
Cage Green Primary School
Duncombe Primary School
Early Foundations Teaching School Alliance
London Borough of Islington Early Years team
Northfleet Nursery
Potential in Everyone Academy Trust
Riverview Primary School
Rosherville Primary School
Shears Green Infant School
The Oaks Infant School

Bernadette Alexiou, Sheba Ahmed, Paula Arriagada, Lauren Bore, Ian Brown, Nicola Chapman, Elsye Crescitelli, Joanne Dove, Elisabet Espinosa, Helen Esdale-Smith, Mireilli Forrest, Maria Garrido, Shona Hathway, Kimberley Holland, Rachel Hollingworth, Salma Khatun, Ayse Korkmaz, Jayne Lilly, Michelle McCormack, Rosalind Munday, Panna Nagar, Karen O'Connor, Catherine Pike, Eloise Ratford-Harris, Sarah Taylor, Daniel Watts, Jenny Wynn.

Higher Education Innovation Funding (HEIF) support for some of these projects was provided by UCL Innovation & Enterprise.

The authors and publisher are grateful for permission to reproduce the following materials in this book:

London Centre for Leadership in Learning (LCLL)

And all those who preferred to remain anonymous; you know who you are, thank you.

Amanda Ince and Eleanor Kitto

Foreword

By Dr. Guy Roberts-Holmes

The purposes, expectations, and understandings of Early Childhood Education and Care (ECEC) are currently undergoing an enormous questioning and change. At the same time, practitioners' and teachers' work and family life can be increasingly precarious and stressful. These personal and wider professional societal changes and pressures upon early childhood can be overwhelming to make sense of, manage, and control. However, it is important that practitioners and teachers do not throw their hands up in despair but rather hold onto the many possibilities and alternatives that exist. It is here that Amanda Ince's and Eleanor Kitto's *A Practical Guide to Action Research and Teacher Inquiry: Making a Difference in Early Years* is such an important and timely book, precisely because it encourages practitioners to engage with child-centred professional possibilities and alternatives. The text is significant, rigorous, and original precisely because it encourages practitioners and teachers to articulate their often deeply held passionate and professional voices through owning their practice through the action research process. The narrative is empowering because *A Practical Guide to Action Research and Teacher Inquiry* demonstrates how practitioners and teachers can find their professional voice and how to make that all important voice heard!

This book is important because early childhood practitioners and teachers are often in a much better position to understand the complexities of children's rights and needs than policy makers far removed from practice. So, being a critically reflective practitioner researcher and engaging with the myriad of possibilities and alternatives of early childhood practice enables you to move beyond simple, reductionist, and technical "fixes", so liked by policymakers. Engaging with the detailed action research examples in this book, practitioners and teachers will be helping with the democratic professionalization of early childhood.

A unique feature of this book is the use of Facilitated Action Research (FAR). Step by step, FAR carefully takes the researchers through the entire action research cycle as if they had an experienced guide and facilitator working next to them. FAR acts as a detailed scaffold for support from start to finish through the use of ten carefully selected case study examples and resources. By creating an in-depth narrative account of early years practitioners and teachers working with facilitators, FAR enables them to confidently carry out their own unique project. By using a FAR approach, this book captures the varied and diverse practitioner and teacher journeys, and so sets out a detailed and successful model on how to undertake their own early years action research projects.

The detailed narrative takes the practitioner through the entire action research cycle from collaboratively identifying a problem to investigate, to collating the information, implementing a change, and evaluating the impact. It is particularly impressive that the book politically centres the participation of young children throughout the entire process. A further very useful feature of the book is the impact evaluation framework that enables the reflective practitioners to catalogue and evidence the differences their research has made once the initial cycle has been made. This book is impressive because it offers access to both the essential basic history and theory of action research, and at the same time enables a deep understanding of critical action research to support high-quality research. As a result, the book is not only relevant to newly qualified early childhood students, practitioners, and teachers, but also offers in-depth insights and inspirations to the more experienced teacher researchers. Dr. Ince's and Dr. Kitto's book makes action research exciting and accessible and inspires the readers to engage in their own important professional development.

By positively taking responsibility for their own professionalization through action research, early childhood practitioners and teachers empower themselves through making democratic, political, and ethical choices. Such democratic decision-making about their own professional work is necessary to defend and extend professional rights and responsibilities at a time when this is under threat. Action research is centrally concerned with practitioners' and teachers' rights to engage in democratic professional decision-making and as such is central to your well-being. Action research is centrally concerned with understanding and making political and ethical choices. Learning to take these political choices and decisions can be transformational in helping early childhood practitioners and teachers to find and articulate their powerful personal and professional voice.

Dr. Guy Roberts-Holmes, Associate Professor, UCL, Institute of Education.

Introduction

This book is written in response to a perceived gap in the information and support available for early years practitioners to carry out small-scale projects in their settings in order to improve provision, practice, and outcomes for children. These projects are sometimes identified as action research, but there is a great variety and some confusion over what that means and how to carry it out. This book aims to provide clarification of what action research in early years particularly might involve. It offers specific practical support on how to plan, implement, and evaluate projects by practitioners using action research and an impact evaluation approach.

Background

The authors have both worked as early years practitioners in various settings and with a range of roles and responsibilities. We are fortunate to have worked with many amazing colleagues and we have noticed a common denominator across all qualification levels from level 2 apprentice to graduate and postgraduate Masters-level students. This is the desire of practitioners in early years settings to make a difference to their practice for the benefit of the children. However, in expressing that desire they have also indicated that it was difficult to access formal professional development and that many courses were generic and not tailored to the specific issues affecting their children and setting. Many practitioners undertake action research projects as part of their initial training. But these projects are usually under the supervision of tutors, supported by taught input and structured resources. These projects provide practitioners with some experience but perhaps not the understanding and deeper knowledge of action research. They appear as more "top down" directed in nature rather than enabling practitioners to "take ownership" and to create projects independently with confidence for their own unique setting and circumstances. A potential result is practitioners end up feeling that they lack confidence and the necessary know-how or current research knowledge to carry out improvements in their context by themselves or as a staff group. An alternative approach was taken in some cases whereby settings were able to engage with tutors or facilitators to work on what the authors identify as "Facilitated Action Research in the Early Years". Feedback and evaluations from those experiences highlighted the value of carrying out action research and the longer term impact for practitioners through increased confidence and the willingness to make changes.

This book is written to address practitioners' concerns by providing the next step in a continuum from taught action research as part of initial qualification at whatever level, via projects facilitated by external experts (tutors/facilitators) to practitioners carrying out projects independently in their own settings and tailored to the needs of their children and context with the aim of creating sustainable communities of learners (Stoll, Harris, & Handscomb, 2012), confident to improve practice, supported by examples and resources.

Aims and objectives

This book aims to act as a scaffold, by breaking down complex ideas and activity into simple achievable steps, for early years practitioners in undertaking action research or teacher enquiry so that they feel confident and empowered to make changes to benefit the children in their setting. Frequently, practitioners identify issues and practices they would like to change. But sometimes they lack the knowledge or confidence and are not sure how best to approach it. This book provides strategies, ideas, and examples to bridge the gap between wanting to make a change or address an issue and making that change.

Why use action research?

Many practitioners undertake action research projects as part of their initial training. This is because action research is recognised as highly effective with a huge body of research supporting its effectiveness in practice (Carr and Kemmis, 1986; McNiff, 2015, Roberts-Holmes, 2018). The action research projects undertaken in early years practitioner training are usually tightly controlled and structured as part of an accredited award. They are often assessed as coursework or linked to placements. Experienced tutors are on hand to advise and mentors or workplace colleagues are available to guide and support. The projects are usually very successful, fun, and worthwhile for all involved. However, undertaking such a project as a lone practitioner without the support network provided by accredited training can be daunting. Continuing professional development is available throughout the sector, but there is currently an emphasis on compliance with a focus on safeguarding, PREVENT strategy, first aid, and updating. As Maria noted: "training offered regular interventions for the last 20 years, but this is something different". The difference is the "facilitated" action research (FAR). There are many texts and research articles about action research and the benefits of teacher enquiry. Although they are readily available, a gap remains between the texts and practice. That gap is the divide between theory and practice, and for early years practitioners that includes knowing how to mediate ideas and suggestions so that they can be adapted and adopted for the particular context in which they work with the individual children they educate and care for. This book bridges that gap by providing a facilitated version of action research. It is a step-by-step guide as though practitioners are working with an experienced facilitator. In fact, that is exactly what happened with the projects in the book. These examples create a narrative account of early years practitioners working with facilitators to carry out projects in their own settings. This book captures those journeys and sets out FAR as a successful approach for individuals and organizations to undertake action research projects in the early years.

The book aims to:

▦ Bridge the gap between pre-service/initial training about teacher enquiry and action research and how to implement a project in practice independently.

▦ Empower practitioners to carry out action research in their own settings by providing a set of resources, strategies, and ideas supported by worked examples for carrying out projects step by step.

▦ Develop practitioner confidence to make changes using an action research cycle approach.

It does this by:

▦ Presenting the action research cycle as a framework for projects. This cycle is broken down into individual stages, each one supported by a clear rationale and examples from practice to illustrate the stages and processes.

▦ Offering tried-and-tested resources that practitioners can use to support each stage of their project. These are provided as templates in the appendices and explained in the text.

▦ Providing examples of action research projects in the early years by real practitioners in real settings with real children.

Organisation of text and how to use it

This book is specifically designed to be used by practitioners at all levels, from level 2 trainees to early years initial teacher training (EYITT) and postgraduate, working within early childhood settings. The book is set out in easy-to-follow sections starting with clear definitions and explanations of action research. These are accompanied by a commentary on how these can be applied to early years settings to address local questions or issues around how to improve outcomes for children. Whilst we would suggest reading the text in its entirety, it is equally possible to utilise the sections separately and explore the examples for inspiration in relation to your own individual context and research priorities.

Part one provides an overview of action research. It begins with an explanation and history of action research. It then moves into considering what action research offers in terms of benefits for settings, individuals, and children. It then considers aspects of the role of "evidence" for informing practice, as there are implications for choices practitioners might make in their projects and the resources and materials they might choose to draw upon to underpin and strengthen their work. This discussion leads into the section on making a difference. A key aspect and motivator for the early years is the desire to improve outcomes and experiences for children. Using an impact evaluation framework is a unique aspect of this text and this is closely linked to being able to evidence a difference made. Finally, this section discusses some of the ethical considerations when undertaking action research and highlights some of the potential conflicts encountered within practitioner research. Part one ends with a summary and leads into a detailed description of each phase of action research in Part two.

Part two is organised into a sequence of five sections, each outlining a specific phase of the action research cycle and is topped and tailed by an introduction and summary. The phases provide a clear guide to the order and content of each phase, enabling practitioners to create their own action research project and work through to successful completion. The stages of action research are illustrated by examples from practice and linked back to the rationale and theory so that there is a guide to not only what to do but, more importantly, why. Further support for each phase is provided by templates and resources available in the appendices to scaffold practitioners in completing their own projects.

Part three is a carefully selected collection of ten examples of early years action research projects. The projects were chosen to showcase a wide variety of topics, settings, and age ranges to provide a practical illustration of how action research by early years practitioners is possible and can be highly effective in developing practice and improving outcomes.

Resources to support each stage of the project are available in the appendices and linked to each chapter. These resources have all been used by practitioners as part of their action research projects as tools to support planning, reflecting, and evaluating their research activity. The resources are offered as prompts, scaffolds, and suggestions to support the thinking processes and to capture the stages of action research and teacher enquiry cycles. They are not designed as prescriptive requirements. We hope they will be useful. And where they have a copyright attached, please respect their use for educational purposes only.

Because a central component of this text is the collaboration between the authors and the participants in facilitated action research in the early years projects, it makes sense to start with the voices of some of the participants in how they view the action research process and the influence that it has had on them, their settings, their practice, and their teams. The voices of participants are also included throughout, as it is hoped that the views of experienced practitioners will help to illustrate the value of each aspect of the action research process.

Part one

Action research: Theory and practice

Introduction

Action research is a term frequently used within the field of education and is a recognised approach for carrying out research. One glossary characterises it as "action research or practitioner research attempts to instigate change in the form of improved practice, policy and culture within an institution. Action research is a collaborative and participatory research approach" (Roberts-Holmes, 2018:xvii). Action research offers a powerful tool in the early-years practitioners' professional repertoire, as it provides a structured approach to exploring, and developing, practice. As outlined by Somekh (1995:340) "action research methodology bridges the divide between research and practice". It provides a framework for practitioners to investigate aspects of practice systematically, make adaptations, and consider the impact of their revisions. Understanding the what, why, and how of action research can empower individuals and settings, potentially raising quality, improving outcomes for children, and acting as a motivator for staff.

This chapter provides the theoretical rationale for engaging in action research within the Early Years Foundation Stage (EYFS). It explains what we mean by action research and how it emerged and came to be used within educational contexts. The chapter then considers some of the many reasons that practitioners choose to engage in action research and presents a discussion on some of the benefits specifically associated with the action research process for professional, personal, and institutional development within the EYFS.

What is action research?

Action research has many definitions throughout a vast literature. It is explained by Manion and Cohen (1994:186) as a "small-scale intervention in the functioning of the real world and the close examination of the effects of such intervention". This definition is particularly useful for considering the process within the EYFS, as it emphasises the focus on making a change and investigating the consequences of that change, within the real, everyday life of a setting. However, the centrality of the practitioner and the importance of self-reflection within the process are less evident within the above definition. McNiff (2002:15) emphasises that "action research is enquiry by the self, into the self…[it] involves learning in and through action and reflection". The practitioner's own learning and consideration of the interconnection between the practitioner and practice when implementing and evaluating change are all essential features of the approach discussed within this text. As a starting point for thinking about the action research process, these are considered core components. However, in order to position these within the broader context, it is useful to consider the history of action research and some of the contentions which contribute to the challenge of establishing a concise definition.

How did action research develop?

Action research, as a term and a concept, is widely cited as having been first developed by Kurt Lewin (1890–1947) in the 1940s. However, Masters (1995) suggests that its origins lay much earlier in the 20th century, and, as the process has continued to develop, there is no singular definition which can be attributed to a particular person at a particular point in time. This sentiment is echoed by Dickens and Watkins (2006:185), who refer to action research as an "umbrella term for a shower of activities intended to foster change". Whilst not wishing to dismiss these views, it is the work of Lewin and subsequent proponents of his conception of action research that forms the central tenets of the approach advocated within this text. It is, therefore, a logical starting point to provide a brief synopsis of the emergence of Lewin's view and the ensuing development of action research within education.

In looking to address sociological challenges specifically concerned with group relations Lewin (1946) noted the need to integrate aspects of the social sciences, psychology, sociology, and social anthropology, in order to better understand, and effect change in, social situations. He asserted that the complexity of social activity required that such changes were most effectively achieved through exploration and action carried out by those social agents most closely concerned with the practices. In contrast to more detached models of research and leadership, Lewin proposed a participatory, collaborative, and democratic approach to exploring and influencing social action.

> The research needed for social practice can best be characterized as research for social management or social engineering. It is a type of action-research, a comparative research on the condition and effects of various forms of social action, and research leading to social action. Research that produces nothing but books will not suffice.
>
> (Lewin, 1946:35)

Lewin problematised that such research, however, would require a set of standards by which to evaluate and measure progress. He presented a cyclical model of "planning, executing, and reconnaissance" applied systematically, in order to monitor and direct focus (Lewin, 1946:38). It is the recurrent cycles, and the role of participants in investigating and directing social action, that made the essence of action research particularly appealing to educational contexts. Action research in these different contexts, from nursery to post-compulsory education settings, reflects the ways in which Lewin's model has been adapted and developed, subsequently leading to a wide variety in form and structure. Lewin's contention that research should be structured, and more than the production of books, has contributed to the current discussion about the role of close-to-practice research and the importance of practitioner agency (Wyse et al., 2018).

The development and application of action research in education

The emergence of action research as a process, according to Adelman (1993), coincided with a growing interest in democratic educational reform. This was promoted by John Dewey (1859–1952), who considered the potential of action research as a tool for actualising practice, built from his fundamental belief in the power of democracy in education at all levels, including practitioners.

The use of action research in education was further popularised by Corey (1954), outlining the specific relevance of the approach for enabling teachers and others to improve their own practices.

> They accumulate evidence to define their problems more sharply. They draw upon all of the experience available to them as a source for action hypotheses that give promise of enabling them to ameliorate or eliminate the practical difficulties of their day by day work. They test out these promising procedures on the job and again accumulate the best evidence they can of their effectiveness.
>
> (Corey, 1954:375)

Corey's statement positions practitioners as central to pedagogic decision-making and identifies their importance in understanding the contextual issues that might be suitable research foci.

The evolution of action research as a process or as an overarching term for a divergent set of methodological or epistemological perspectives (Peters & Robinson, 1984; McNiff, 2013; McAteer, 2014) continued in different academic disciplines and different social spheres. Within UK education, action research gained momentum and validity. This was through the works of Lawrence Stenhouse, who emphasised the role of practitioners in schools as central to the development of educational research (Stenhouse, 1981), and John Elliott, who propagated the development of "a reflective culture in which teaching strategies are perceived as potentially problematic and therefore objects of reflective deliberation in particular contexts" (Elliott, 1991:111).

With the impetus to "improve the quality of education and give teachers an enhanced role in shaping educational policy and school reform" John Elliott founded the Classroom Action Research Network in 1976 (later to become the Collaborative Action Research Network, or CARN). This was intended to facilitate connection between teacher researchers and promote "action and research as integrated activities, in which educational reform is informed by research knowledge generated in local contexts *by* teachers and *with* teachers, not *on* teachers" (Somekh, 2010:105).

The central features of action research in contemporary educational settings remain those of cycles of exploratory, self-reflective interrogation of contextually embedded practices, undertaken by practitioners for practitioners. This enables action research to be applied to a very broad range of contexts for a broad range of purposes. However, the flexibility of action research and the breadth of its scope can be viewed both as its strength and its limitation, whilst the key components of self-reflective, practitioner-directed exploration can be viewed as the emancipatory underpinning of the action research process for educational reform. This is in contrast to other approaches to educational research. It is also the personalised, individual principle of the approach which, arguably, inhibits the development of a "cumulative body of knowledge" that might contribute to the broader view of evidence-based practice, and, consequently, truly satisfy the vision of the founders of action research (Hargreaves, 2007a:51). In addition to the challenge of how individual endeavours can contribute to a broader dialogue about practice, the popularity of action research has resulted in a vast array of differing definitions and interpretations of what constitutes an appropriate approach. It is our contention that education per se is such a broad and multifarious notion, and that action research is such a flexible tool, that no singular body of knowledge could be amassed which might be sufficiently reciprocally beneficial to practitioner-researchers within education as a broad field. It is for that reason we have attempted to initiate a shared framework specifically relevant for conducting action research within early years settings and provide a forum for sharing accumulated experiences. It is our view that practitioners are the experts and, as such, have much to contribute to a discourse about developing practice, but that this is best facilitated through some aspect of shared process and shared focus. It is for this reason that we have developed specific phases for an action research cycle in the EYFS, as outlined through this book in Part two and exemplified through real life action research projects in Part three. It is not, however, our intention to be so prescriptive that we detract from the original goals of the concept of action research. To this end, the most concise definition of action research, from our perspective, is that offered by Kemmis (2007):

> Action research is a form of self-reflective enquiry undertaken by participants in social (including educational) situations in order to improve the rationality and justice of (a) their own social or educational practices, (b) their understanding of these practices, and (c) the situations in which the practices are carried out.
>
> (p. 168)

Why engage in action research in the early years?

Practitioners say: ...

"It makes you see things in a different way".
"It makes you think about practice and organisation".

One of the founding principles of action research is the development of practice through "democratic participation rather than autocratic coercion" (Adelman, 1993:7). In addition, although not essential, Kemmis (2007:168) suggests that "it is most rationally empowering when undertaken by participants collaboratively". This egalitarian, collaborative approach to investigating practice and effecting change, is what, in our opinion, makes the action research process so applicable to early years settings. In educational contexts where conflicting priorities are often directing practices, establishing a professional dialogue to explore and develop practices offers a means by which pedagogical decision making can be shared and justified. In a context where, one would hope, all adults have a shared resolve to enhance the short- and long-term futures of the children in their care, constructing collaborative investigations into aspects of practice offers opportunities to expose and unify the perspectives that shape activity. Collaboration, both within and between settings, has potential to further strengthen the dedicated community of early years practitioners. It provides support and challenge, as well as advancing a shared repertoire with which to advocate for the best interests of children, amidst the myriad of outsider perspectives on "good practice". Put simply, engaging in action research offers personal and professional satisfaction for individuals in addressing an issue within the setting. Working to resolve the issue in order to enhance the outcomes or experience for children resonates with Fullan and Ballew's (2004) "moral purpose" and the desire of many in early years settings "to make a difference".

What is in it for me?

Practitioners say: ...

"It made me really think about what interested me in the field and how I could improve my practice".
"I was able to reflect on my own practice and use my strengths to make a change".

Individuals and teams engage in action research for a variety of reasons. Sometimes it is in response to external pressures, internal challenges, or personal motivations.

At the crux, though, is a personal decision that justifies the commitment to a project on top of the normal EYFS workload. That decision is informed by a range of factors and, either consciously or unconsciously, the weighing up of "what is in it for me?" against the potential challenges.

One key reason for engaging in action research is the sense of ownership over practice that it engenders. It can be easy, within a busy early years setting, to adopt practices without a particular rationale for doing so. Reasons for practices being undertaken in a particular way can sometimes be justified in terms of *"that's how we do it here"* or *"it has always been done this way"*. Whereas, engaging in action research, interrogating ideas, and establishing procedures which have been explored and evaluated provide practitioners with a narrative for directing and justifying aspects of their own practice and provision. This sense of ownership offers positive repercussions, just for the development of practice but also the development of individuals.

The following key factors have provided the rationales for practitioners' decisions to participate and have been used to support settings in discussing whether to commit to action research as an approach. These are not presented in a priority order, as the importance of each varies according to the context and individuals involved. As broad categories, the benefits of action research within the EYFS can be considered in relation to "professional development", "team development", and "children's development".

Professional development

> **Practitioners say: ...**
>
> *"The Action Research Project helped me to see ways to further my professional development".*
> *"I was very lucky to be able to take part in the action research and feel that it has boosted my confidence".*

The nature of action research, as self-reflective enquiry undertaken by practitioners with a view to improving their own practice, implies that professional development is central to the process. Action research is identified as a professional development activity, with some organisations allowing staff that engage in action research projects to count these towards performance management, training, and self-development targets. Its worth lies in reflecting on one's own practice, gaining new insights, and making changes. Its value as "a chance to consolidate existing skills and develop new ones" (General Teaching Council for England, 2006:5) makes it attractive as a way of developing personally and professionally. Furthermore, McNiff (2002:15) emphasises that "it is a form of research which can be undertaken in any context, regardless of ... status or position".

Some argue that professional learning is a more accurate term to employ than training or professional development. In this book we recognise those arguments and adopt Porritt's (2013:79) view that "professional development should mean that teachers and leaders have changed and improved their existing practice as a result of engaging in professional learning". With this in mind, we use the terminology adopted by the practitioners whose comments and projects are included. For example, a much used cliché about undertaking any type of learning or development is one of the journey, and yet that view resonates strongly with practitioners undertaking action research, with Maria explaining: "It's something that takes you on a journey, you wonder what it is, but once you start, you think, oh that makes sense". This transformational element is an important aspect and is embedded in the approaches we take within this text and in the Facilitated Action Research projects.

Research highlights the importance of being up to date with current thinking and practice and that professional development opportunities can act as factors in retaining and recruiting staff into a sector that suffers from low status and pay (European Union, 2013). It is also crucial in providing the quality workforce that Nutbrown (2012) characterises as essential for quality provision. As a result, action research is often welcomed as a fun and helpful way for practitioners to make changes and develop their own skills and abilities professionally and personally.

Team development

Practitioners say: ...

"It has had a great impact to actually be more reflective on our practice and exchange ideas with the team".

"It is nice to meet with colleagues to discuss practice and have a positive impact on the children and environment".

One of the many features, and arguably one of the main benefits, of action research is its capacity for making the implicit explicit. When working in teams throughout the EYFS we can all make assumptions about the shared understanding, beliefs, and perspectives that colleagues and teams hold. It is only by voicing our views and establishing an atmosphere where all feel at ease in voicing their opinions that differing outlooks can be identified and professionally debated. The process of exploring differing views and, potentially, reconciling pedagogical priorities within teams can be illuminating, but it requires an egalitarian philosophy towards the exchange of perspectives. A climate for pedagogical discussion requires that all members of a team feel confident to express their perspectives, feel comfortable in questioning their own viewpoint, or questioning the viewpoint of others, and feel open to adopting new ways of thinking. The methods applied in attempting to develop this will be heavily dependent on the existing climate within a setting and the extent to which this philosophy is already embedded within the context. For many settings embarking upon an action research project as a team, establishing, and maintaining, some core principles for collaborative discussion will be necessary. These principles should build from the notion of democracy, where all perspectives are valuable and all views are open to scrutiny. This is premised on Kemmis's (2013:167) view that "action research is a participatory democratic form of educational research for educational improvement". Democratic discussion can be challenging, particularly in settings where structured hierarchies exist. However, once established, this process of collective thinking can also provide a shared rationale for decision-making in areas beyond the action research focus. In busy EYFS environments, it can often be difficult to dedicate time to collective discussion within teams. Establishing a shared repertoire for negotiating perspectives on practice can facilitate the ongoing development of pedagogical dialogue and contribute to team cohesion through continual collective reflection upon practice. Creating a shared focus through the development of an action research project supports teams with opportunities to have such discussion and reflection. The importance of collaborative discussion is highlighted in the examples provided in Part two and reflected upon by participants who shared their experiences of the process.

Children's development

Practitioners say: …

"Using pupil voice really helped us to see things from the children's perspective and enabled us to make informed decisions".
"It is encouraging the children to engage with one another, sharing stories, and taking turns".

It is likely that one of the main motivations for engaging in action research is the potential impact that it offers to children's development, through the development of provision and practice. However, irrespective of initial motivation for engaging in the action research process, its emphasis upon addressing individual aspects of practice relevant to individual settings by nature has influence on the provision, and subsequently the outcomes for the children. It is our firm belief that it is the practitioners within a setting that are the experts on the children and the interpersonal dynamics of the provision. The action research process enables practitioners to use their expertise to consider the individual experiences of children in their context and investigate aspects of the provision equipped with insights into the specific histories and priorities of children participating within that context. From our experience, it is often the case that outcomes for specific individuals, or groups, form the initial impetus for practitioners wanting to investigate aspects of their provision. However, it has been a recurring theme that these investigations have led to the development of practices which have been beneficial for all.

It is our experience that EYFS practitioners, in roles at all levels, have the well-being and development of the children at the centre of all that they do. By engaging in the action research process, interconnecting their own investigations with wider perspectives from the literature, practitioners are able to harness this and shape provision which is firmly based on the understanding of the individuals within it. This is evidenced throughout the practitioners' narratives about their action research projects. For example, one practitioner commented that "it broadened my knowledge with regard to where our target group wanted us to take their learning", another commented that "we were able to think about how ideas in our readings related to our children particularly, to enable us to make changes with them in mind". Other examples are captured throughout this text and, these comments, highlight the moral purpose that drives early years practitioners in continuously improving for the sake of the children. However, it is important that practitioners feel that the changes being made are likely to result in positive outcomes for children. After all, any change will have an impact, the key is to make an impact that is positive and will have a greater influence than the mere passage of time. For example, if children improve their physical skills, is this because they are now slightly older and have developed these skills naturally, or is the physical skill level more than would be expected naturally in that time frame and as a result of interventions by practitioners. One way to support the decision-making process about what changes and why is for practitioners to engage with research. Research can provide evidence for particular ways of working, resources, and interventions. Key for early years is thinking about whether this evidence is credible and helpful in relation to practice.

Evidence-informed practice

Practitioners say: …

"It was great to have time to reflect upon practice. Being able to access research was informative for the whole team".

"Having a focus for engaging with literature made the process of searching for articles less daunting".

Since Hargreaves's (1996) call for a partnership between researchers and practitioners to be at the heart of reform in educational research, discussion around the interconnections between research and practice has been ongoing (Elliott, 2007; Hammersley, 2007; Hargreaves, 2007a;). However, Kemmis (2007:173) is very clear in his argument that "action research is [as] the study of praxis", that is, their own practice. These arguments are part of the bigger debate about how to close the research to practice gap. This gap can be polarised by researchers claiming they have the answers if only practitioners could understand and would adopt and implement their research, whilst practitioners argue that such systematic research is not applicable in the real world and the specific contexts in which they operate. Moreover, practitioners claim that such research is not accessible and easily available as it is published in academic journals. These arguments are across a range of fields and not confined to education. To bring these polarised positions together in efforts to close the research to practice gap and to help practitioners make informed decisions based on credible sources, evidence-based practice has emerged. In the field of education, it can be defined as follows:

> evidence-based practice in education as a decision-making process that integrates (1) the best available evidence, (2) professional judgment, and (3) client values and context.
>
> (Spencer, Dietrich, & Slocum, 2012:129)

The focus on professional judgement as a core factor in the decision-making process has led to another term being used – evidence-informed practice.

The notions of *evidence-based* and *evidence-informed* practices are often, contentiously, distinguished by the freedom or limitation of interpretation of evidence in differing contexts. However, this distinction is largely semantic and somewhat misleading. It is argued that all research requires interpretation and, consequently, the suggestion that research findings can simply be adopted is, therefore, illogical. Hargreaves (1999) made the distinction, in part, in response to criticism of the positivist perspective projected through the notion of "evidence-based" practice. Acknowledging that:

> Decisions are not based on research evidence alone; the evidence is but one (albeit important) element in decision making, which also has to take into account a range of unique contextual factors …. To avoid any implication that teachers or educational policy makers should not, in making decisions, take account of (i) the quality and strength of the research evidence and (ii) the contextual factors relating to that decision, we should, I suggest, speak of evidence-informed, not evidence-based, policy or practice.
>
> (Hargreaves, 1999:246)

Ongoing debates remain about the extent to which education could be evidence-informed or evidence-based, or, indeed, whether either notion could be achieved or desired (Biesta, 2010). However, it is substantially important that EYFS practitioners undertaking action research critically engage with literature to consider the aspect of practice that is the focus of their investigations.

It could be argued that "evidence" is available to support any pedagogical position. The extent to which such evidence is relevant to a specific context would be dependent upon the individual perspectives, the institutional priorities, and the political climate at any point in time. Whilst we would not advocate merely adopting a particular perspective from the literature, or adopting a particular approach simply because somebody somewhere says that it is "effective", it is through critical engagement with wider views that practitioners can position their own practice, explore their own beliefs, and develop a shared repertoire for considering aspects of their provision.

Timperley and Earl (2008) identify conditions for evidence-informed conversations that, they suggest, are necessary for interpreting and utilising evidence for educational improvement. The first condition relates to the relevance of the evidence to the work of the practitioners, the second is the need for an "inquiry habit of mind", and the third concerns the balance between respect and challenge. They argue that inquiry-based conversations that include these conditions facilitate the shared meaning that precipitates evidence-informed action. From this view, the relevance of evidence, an authentic interest in developing understanding, and the interpersonal dynamics of the discussion group all influence the interpretation and use of evidence (Timperley & Earl, 2008).

Similarly, with a particular focus upon professional learning communities within the EYFS, Brown and Rogers (2015) examined the use of "knowledge-creation activity", through collaboration between experts with tacit practice-based knowledge and those with *formal* knowledge for establishing meaningful evidence use (Brown & Rogers, 2015). From this perspective, it could be argued that the facilitated action research in the early years projects also constitutes "knowledge-creation activity". This is by virtue of the combination of practitioner expertise and a rigorous action research framework, echoing the recent BERA "Close to practice inquiry" (BERA, 2018a).

There are many starting points when sourcing literature or research evidence for supporting discussions and investigations. The Sutton Trust, an educational charity that supports educational research, and the Education Endowment Fund (EEF) online toolkit offers one approach to support practitioners considering options. The toolkit rates interventions and approaches on the basis of research evidence available, the rigor of that evidence, and the cost of the implementation. The toolkit takes a "what works" stance and reflects a more quantitative evidence base. This means it highlights data and statistics in reporting outcomes and the potential usefulness of the intervention. In early years research a more qualitative approach is often used, particularly for small-scale research which seeks to understand the individual detail. However, the EEF toolkit provides a guide and may save time by helping practitioners dismiss approaches that are both costly and less effective and focus on those that might be more supportive or relevant for their context. The toolkit was consulted by some participants in projects discussed later in this text.

It is important to realise that engaging in reading and research literature itself will not make the decision about what to do for practitioners. After all, practitioners:

> are not going to be given a recipe for what works from research; by its nature, educational research cannot provide certainty of outcome. What it can achieve is to provide reasonable warrant for decisions that must be taken by teachers, in full knowledge of the circumstances in which they work.
>
> (Winch, Oancea, & Orchard, 2015:210)

Therefore, the combined knowledge of the practitioners and their professional judgements in light of the needs of their children is crucial to interpret research and its importance within the decision-making process. So, a more nuanced view is required that goes beyond a simplistic one-size-fits-all policy approach of "this works, do it", which is sometimes promoted. The responsibility is passed back to the practitioners to carefully and critically reflect on what works for whom in what circumstances, as well as how this relates to their children in their context and their practices.

Making the difference: Planning your project with impact evaluation

Practitioners say: ...

"Evaluating the impact of the research enabled us to justify our changes and articulate how the action research project had influenced practice".

"The impact wasn't just in the changes to the environment. It was within us, as a team, and within me, as a teacher".

The key to successful projects is reflecting throughout each stage on changes made and whether these changes have had any impact. Understanding how to think about impact can be daunting, and in the next section we provide a helpful guide to one way of considering the difference your project is making by using an approach called impact evaluation.

Impact evaluation is a specific way of thinking about your project. The version adopted in this book is predicated on the work of Vivienne Porritt and the London Centre for Leadership and Learning based at the UCL Institute of Education, which in itself is informed by previous research (Kirkpatrick, 1959; Guskey, 2000; Bubb & Earley, 2007; Coldwell & Simkins, 2011). This long history suggests that evaluation is important in a variety of ways, but in educational practice it is sometimes seen as problematic and challenging. This may be because there is a potential lack of time and importance attached to it, or perhaps we are not sure how best to approach evaluation. This is understandable given the external pressures and high-stakes assessment agenda associated with evaluation in early years (Bradbury & Roberts-Holmes, 2017).

Input- or output-based evaluation

There are two approaches for evaluation: input-based and output-based. Taking an input-based approach usually results in counting; for example, counting how many people attended development, how many training events? Who went? How did they score it? The focus is on what is done, rather than what happened. These measures can be helpful but are not useful when thinking about whether the difference you planned to make has been achieved. The old adage "weighing a pig doesn't tell you how good the bacon is" might be said to sum up the input-based approach. If all attendees rate the continuing professional development (CPD) event as excellent, it seems like a good result and indicates a CPD event that has had an impact. However, if they rated it highly because it was a day out of school, they got a good lunch, finished early, and liked the presenter, the effectiveness or impact of the CPD event is likely to be low because none of that information says anything about the learning and how they might change their attitudes or behaviours or what they will do as a result of that input.

Example 1 of input-based evaluation: A nursery wants to encourage parental engagement to support children's learning. They put on a welcome event for parents, there is a parent nursery contact book, they hold a coffee morning, and they create a nursery newsletter. At the end they evaluate their parental engagement project. They have done lots of things (input), but there is limited, if any, impact on levels and quality of parental engagement and its influence on children's learning.

Alternatively, an output-based approach to evaluation focusses on the outcomes in terms of learners, usually children in this context and the benefits they receive from the project. Linked to Guskey's model (2000) of five levels of impact focussing on participants' reactions, learning, organisation support and change, participants' use of new knowledge and skills, and student learning outcomes, the output approach is more useful. It also considers the changes and impact on practitioners; have they changed as a professional and in their practice from engaging in learning? Considering the evaluation of impact specifically in relation to the CPD activity, Earley and Porritt (2010) highlight the importance of identifying and planning for impact in relation to *products, processes, and outcomes*. Products are tangible results of the work and might not be new but will be improved. For example, a newsletter, policy, handbook, staff directory, CPD opportunities catalogue, website, and workshop. Processes are improved or new systems and procedures. For example, a new way of applying for CPD opportunities as offered in the CPD catalogue system for tracking parental engagement. Outcomes or impact is the difference made. It might be to behaviours, attitudes, feelings, skills, or practice. But it also relates to the difference in learning and experience of staff and children as a result of a change in practice (Earley & Porritt, 2010:8).

Example 2 takes an output-based impact evaluation approach using the same focus of parental engagement.

An output-based impact evaluation example: A nursery wants to encourage parental engagement to support children's learning.

Products baseline: Our original practice was: A nursery-home contract.	**Products impact**: Our improved practice will be: An improved policy with a specific parental engagement strategy created with parents.
Processes baseline: Our original practice was: First Tuesday of every term coffee morning. Termly hard copy reports.	**Processes impact**: Our improved practice will be: A more flexible range of times and dates to suit parents unable to attend the coffee morning. More regular electronic progress updates which parents can respond to online (secure data site).
Impact/outcomes: What we were doing originally: Parents felt excluded and found it hard to conform to the nursery expectations (e.g. coffee morning difficult for those in full-time employment). Some parents were unsure of what to do if they wanted to ask questions about the curriculum or how to help their children.	**Impact**: The impact we will have: Parents feel more included and willing to engage. Staff feel they are working with parents in partnership. Staff/parent workshops, e.g. parents skilled in baking make cakes with children, and staff provides commentary on the learning happening to support children's learning with parents who might bake at home. Staff improve baking skills/repertoire of recipes, parents feel more confident about what children are learning by baking. Children enjoy baking.

But to really understand the impact/outcomes, it is important to evaluate the situation prior to embarking upon any activity, as that will assist in providing a benchmark for evaluation at the end (Earley & Porritt, 2010). In Part two we provide advice and guidance on how to do this.

Ethical considerations

One significant dimension in any research is the evaluation of the ethical considerations. This can be particularly challenging with practitioner research, as there is often information available to practitioners as part of their specific role, which, when used for research purposes, requires different consents. It is important to consider the details of existing permissions and the extent to which any data is being used for the purposes that it was collected. This is particularly important for compliance with General Data Protection Regulation (GDPR). Openness and transparency are essential on what you are doing, what you are using, and what your intentions are.

The British Educational Research Association (BERA) provides detailed guidance on ethics in all aspects of educational research. It is suggested that anyone undertaking action research project should consider their own research activity in relation to the "Ethical Guidelines for Educational Research" (BERA, 2018). Similarly, the European Early Childhood Education Research Association (EECERA) provides an "Ethical Code for Early Childhood Researchers" (EECERA, 2015).

A further dimension when considering action research includes the ethical decisions involved in the rationale for your project choices. As the action research process and the decision to engage with it are generally motivated by a desire to explore an aspect of provision that causes challenge with a view to improving it, there is a potential ethical dilemma to choosing whether or not to address the issues causing challenge. For example, you might identify a challenge that, in your view, is adversely affecting children or their outcomes and well-being. Making a decision not to attempt to address the issue could, potentially, be considered unethical.

In a climate where social policies are arguably disconnected and lacking a clear ethical dimension (Powell, 2012), the consequences of conflicting priorities can be disjointed messages around ethical practice in early childhood education and care. As operational leaders of practice, it is assumed that all practitioners are guided by some interpretation of children's "best interests". However, in organisational structures without clear, shared values, it can be difficult to determine these amid a myriad of competing perspectives. This highlights the need for each and every practitioner to assume individual responsibility in considering ethical practice in early childhood, even in the absence of an established and shared ethos (Palaiologou, 2012).

Summary

Action research has been widely applied within educational contexts for the development of practice and exploration of local issues. There are many representations and interpretations of the action research process. From its inception, it has had a cyclical framework for investigating, planning, acting, and evaluating social activity at its core. The view of action research as a form of self-reflective enquiry, which is undertaken by practitioners for practitioners is, in our view, particularly useful in the EYFS, enabling practitioners to utilise their wealth of expertise to explore aspects of practice and influence sustained change.

Within the EYFS, using the action research process provides a tool for investigating, and ultimately addressing, aspects of provision for the benefit of the provision (by which we include staff, children, physical environments, linguistic environments, emotional environments, and the multifaceted interaction between each for constructing the pedagogical surroundings that influence learning and development). The interconnection between practitioner expertise, contextualised investigations, and engagement with wider literature enables pedagogic decision-making to be evidence-informed and contextually meaningful.

The action research process supports the development of individuals and teams, in addition to practice, provision, and outcomes for children. Embedding the evaluation of these transformations into the process provides a shared frame with which to reflect upon practice and contribute to an ongoing narrative.

Part two
The phases of action research

Introduction

This chapter provides a comprehensive step-by-step discussion of the different stages common within the action research process. Each phase overview connects back to the theoretical rationale and provides a detailed discussion of its purpose as well as potential. The chapter uses real examples from a wide variety of action research projects undertaken within Early Years Foundation Stage (EYFS) settings to exemplify the breadth of possibilities as well as the challenges encountered and overcome when enacted within EYFS settings.

The cyclical feature of action research is not a neat, organised, singular process. The cycles can be thought of in different levels. We present a large cycle – identify a focus, collate information, plan and implement a change, evaluate impact, and consider the future. However, underlying each of these stages is a further cycle – plan,

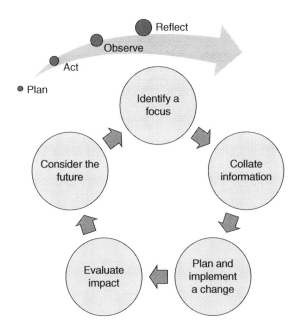

act, observe, and reflect. Both aspects of the process are likely to require more than one rotation in order to investigate the current situation, determine potential aspects for development, and evaluate the consequences of the implemented changes. The precise quantity of revolutions through the plan, act, observe, review cycle within each stage of the larger process will be dependent on the individual context and the area of provision under investigation. The flexibility of action research is one of its key features, so these stages are intended to guide thinking, not dictate it.

Identifying a focus

The initial identification of an aspect of the provision/practice requiring closer scrutiny may well be based on feelings or suspicions rather than determined through more tangible information. One of the features of the action research process is to apply scrutiny to our own tacit beliefs, starting from a general sense of unease about an aspect of practice or a general interest in an area of the provision is perfectly valid. That said, it is also important to remain open-minded in determining the focus. Being aware of our own view as merely one perspective is essential for maintaining the objectivity necessary for authentic critical reflection. If undertaking the research process collaboratively, with other colleagues, then this initial stage is particularly valuable for exploring the breadth of views surrounding aspects of provision and practice. It is also valuable for exploring the range of pedagogical perspectives that influence practitioners' views, but this is only possible if democratic foundations are established from the outset and all participants understand their views are of equal value.

Whilst for some there may be an obvious starting point for investigation, a specific aspect of the provision that seems to need consideration, for others there may be a less clear initial object to explore. Whether there is an obvious or vague starting point, it is useful to expand the question to interrogate interconnected factors that are motivating the current situation and also to question how much influence you have on the situation. Obtaining as broad an initial view of the current situation as possible will support the development of the research process and enable you to refine your focus through the plan, act, observe, and reflect cycle. To support these initial contemplations about the area of focus for initial enquiry, the "Identifying a focus" template (Appendix I) may prove useful for framing your initial thoughts.

Example from practice 1 …

One setting wanted to investigate aspects of their provision that particularly supported imaginative play, with a view to exploring ways to maximise opportunities for children's participation. They were aware that some children didn't choose to

(continued)

engage with the role-play area within the provision, so wanted to facilitate imaginative play in other areas. They started with the question – *Where do children play imaginatively?* In scrutinising their question and sharing it with other practitioners, they realised that the question limited answers to investigating areas where specific types of play were already happening. In recognition of their actual intention of identifying ways to encourage/support imaginative play, they adapted their research questions to be – *How can we facilitate imaginative play episodes throughout the provision?* This enabled practitioners to explore the existing situation as a basis for collaboratively considering how best to support activity through resources and interactions.

Example from practice 2 …

Northfleet Nursery was interested in children's physical development and in particular how gross motor skills fed into finer motor skills and how to support the development of those associated with early writing. They also noticed that children found it difficult to sit still in group carpet time. Children sometimes sat too close to each other or toppled over, causing distress to those they accidentally touched. Initially, they planned a project around developing gross motor skills for writing, targeting boys. In thinking about their focus, they then thought about children that needed more control over their physical movements before drilling down to finer motor movements. Their initial research question became: How can we encourage good gross motor control of children's bodies?

They did some initial research investigating current trends in Early Years practice. This included looking at the Education Endowment Trust (EEF) toolkit to see what might be both cost effective and potentially provide positive outcomes. Yoga for children emerged as a possibility. Originally, they planned to work with a small group of boys who were noticeably less co-ordinated than peers. An initial project introducing basic yoga moves as part of their carpet time routine was so successful that yoga has become a popular part of the weekly nursery routine for all staff and children.

Example from practice 3 …

One setting received funding from the parent association to develop their outdoor area. They decided to make this the focus for their project. Developing the outdoor area is a wide focus so reflecting on what aspects, the budget available, timeline and what might be reasonably achieved, why they felt it important to develop this area, and who it would benefit helped to shape the focus. Practitioners identified a group of summer-born boys who couldn't wait to be outside, but once there fought over limited scooters and chose to engage in a restricted range of activities.

(continued)

Combining this with setting data on early writing helped practitioners to focus on utilising the children's enthusiasm for outdoor learning by developing the outdoor writing environment. Their focus became how to develop the outdoor learning environment for summer-born boys (although other children would be involved and would benefit) to develop early writing.

Ask a question

Asking a question is a good way of thinking about your focus in a way that leads to change. Questions you might ask are "what?" and "why?" "What is the issue or area that I am interested in? Why does it interest me or matter?" These questions might be expanded to consider who would benefit from a change. Maybe there are individuals you have noticed or groups that need more or seem less engaged, motivated, or interested in learning in some way. Often changes or ideas in response to a need from one child or small group positively benefit all. Sometimes thinking about specific children or groups makes it easier to refine the focus and to consider the project as manageable. Considering a change for the entire setting might initially be overwhelming. Many projects start small but expand over the duration of the project or lead to further developments in the future. Or as Handscombe and McBeath (2003:3) suggest, "it is about turning intuitive and spontaneous judgements into more systematic investigations, and it starts with the everyday questions that teachers ask themselves".

Taking these everyday questions and turning them into research questions to address through an action research project needs a little thought. It is important to be realistic in setting your focus. It also needs to be something that you are sufficiently interested in to commit time and effort to. Ideally there will be a focus that you and colleagues can share as working collaboratively is part of the power of action research as well as being easier and more fun.

What makes a good enquiry question?

The London Centre for Leadership in Learning (LCLL) provides some helpful prompts for formulating questions that work well for action research projects.

- Create a question that is open-ended enough to allow possibilities to emerge.

- Try to avoid "yes" and "no" type questions.

- Consider using questions that begin with "how" or "why" or "under what circumstances/conditions".

- It is usually more helpful to investigate broader issues that affect a group rather than an individual.

(continued)

▨ Will it enhance your practice?

▨ Is it really doable in the time you have?

▨ Is it really and truly of personal and professional importance to you?

(Copyright LCLL, 2008)

Once you have formulated a question it is helpful to play "devil's advocate" with it. Ask colleagues or friends to help or become a ruthless objective prober of your own question. The aim is to critique your question to refine it so that you can be confident you have a question that is SMART. By that we mean specific; measurable in some way; realistic in terms of time, resources, and aim; and targeted. It is often easier to spot issues with other people's questions than it is to see the flaws in your own. For example, do you agree with the critique of the question below? Using the prompts on what make a good question, how might you reframe it to make it more appropriate and suitable for an action research project?

Critiquing a question:

Can boys be taught in ways that best address their more active natures?
  This question sets up a "yes" or "no" answer. It also makes several assumptions about boys (do they have different natures to girls? if there are differences, what are they?) and begs the question "what does 'best' in this context mean?" Is it a good idea to teach boys and girls differently? Do age groups matter here? These issues mean that it is not a well-formulated question and will lead to difficulties if adopted for an action research project.

It can be challenging to objectively reflect on your own question and to critique it. By that we mean ask awkward questions, probe, and unpick in detail exactly what it means. It is easier to spot errors, mistakes, oversights, and assumptions in other people's work than our own. We tend to read what we want it to say or intended, rather than what it is; we all do it, and that is why editors are so essential to the writing process. But in research and action research, editors are not available, and training yourself to be sufficiently objective, critical, and able to see what is really written is hard. A quick way forward is to work collaboratively with colleagues, using a "critical friend" approach to refine your question. Below is an activity which works well in developing the "critical friend" approach and enables research questions to be honed successfully. It involves sharing your question with colleagues by writing it on paper and passing it round and asking them to critique it. Each colleague or group writes a further question or comment about the proposed research question using a different colour pen. The questions and comments require the originator to reflect and address the comments, ultimately refining the question into one that seems viable. This leads to the next stage of the process, collating information.

How do you know they are reluctant?

How are you determining whether or not they are "engaged"?

What makes them "reluctant"?

How can we engage reluctant writers?

Are the children reluctant writers when independent or when completing a given task?

"Reluctant" assumes a deficit model.

What writing opportunities already exist in the provision?

Collating information—Check assumptions, investigate the reality

This element of the process is particularly important for questioning or confirming the initial assumptions about your particular area of focus. In the busy world of early years practice, it can be easy to make quick judgements about particular issues or situations. Collating information provides valuable support for your initial ideas and ensures that in identifying a research question to address through the project, you are working to resolve the reality rather than perceived issue.

Example from practice 1 ...

Staff in a Reception Class were concerned with the perceived lack of oral language exhibited by a large proportion of the class. The school had a high percentage of children with English as an Additional Language (EAL) with a large number of families qualifying for Free School Meals (FSM) although it was in an affluent neighbourhood. They decided to undertake an action research project in Reception to address this situation. They formulated their assumption about oral language into a research question: "How can we address the developmental delay in oral language for Reception Class children?" Working with an external facilitator they were asked to collate information about the children using observations, transition records, and school attainment data to create a clear picture of the current situation for these children. Reviewing the data as a team and sharing observations and impressions they realised that the children were not developmentally delayed in their oral language. Instead there were insufficient opportunities for the children to demonstrate and develop their oral language. The focus changed, and a new research question was formulated leading to a successful project and improved outcomes for children.

Collating information also provides a basis upon which to evaluate progress as the cycles continue. Whilst self-reflection on one's own practice inevitably entails some elements of intuition and personal perspective, unsubstantiated beliefs alone are insufficient. This element of the process enables you to explore your initial views in greater detail, having already established a broad area of focus for scrutinising.

Potential alternative sources of information ...

Consider all available sources of information in and linked to your setting. Don't forget to include parental views, children's voices as well as the more formalised data from established systems such as Tracking data, EYFS Profiles, transition records, home school liaison books, observations (narrative, social, time frame, indoor and outdoor), samples of work, photographs, video/film clips. You may also have samples of children's speech captured on digital recorders or on sticky notes. Your own reflections and evaluations on activities can be useful sources of information too. In some cases, you may want to carry out specific audits (e.g. learning environment or adult-child interactions), or activities such as interviews (structured/unstructured), or questionnaires to create a type of baseline for the start of the project. In some cases, commercially produced resources may provide a helpful way of collecting and collating information. Although if considered, these need to be adopted with a critical eye.

Appendix II offers a helpful framework for thinking about the evidence or data (another way of talking about information) that you might have. It helps you think about and record what that data is, where it is (i.e. electronic records or piece of work in a child's record), and who else might have data/information that would help you in understanding the current situation so that you can be sure that your focus is relevant and your question suitable. It also helps you to plan what else you might need to collect to ensure you have the full picture. For example, this might include setting up a focus group with parents, an activity with children to gain their thoughts, or carrying out an audit with colleagues on provision or quality of interactions.

Example from practice 2 ...

One setting had identified that their EYFS profile data suggested anomalies in children's outcomes in the area of Understanding the World compared to other Areas of Learning. They assumed that this suggested that their provision wasn't supporting children's development in this area and decided to make this a focus for their action research investigations. They set out to work as a staff team on considering how this Area of Learning could be further supported within the provision. In initially considering the potential causes of the data anomalies, their early discussions highlighted differences

(continued)

amongst the team in perspectives on what constituted "acceptable evidence" against the Early Learning Goal. These initial discussions resulted in a broadening of their research focus to explore processes for collecting and interpreting evidence of attainment in all Areas of Learning. Interrogation of their initial focus enabled them to "dig down" further to explore factors that were, potentially, influencing the more apparent challenges. Consequently, they were able to consider ways to address these factors and develop their assessment practices more broadly.

Once you have identified the focus and confirmed the situation through investigating the reality and drawing upon a range of sources of data and information, you will have created a suitable research question. Now you are ready to plan the changes you want to make in order to address the issue identified in the question. Maintaining openness to reconsidering ideas throughout all aspects of the process, through continual reflection, remains essential.

Example from practice 3 …

Staff within a setting providing education and care for two- to three-year-olds had been concerned that the children were not choosing to access the book area within their provision. They initially set out with a research question designed to explore ways to develop the area—"*how can we develop the book area to make it more inviting to the children?*" As a team, they discussed ways to develop the book area and independently researched various examples of themed reading area designs to bring back to the group. They also used a form of time sampling to investigate how frequently children did access the area, with a view to repeating this following the development of the area, to provide comparative data. They spoke with the children to explore their ideas for ways to develop the space, based on images that they had sourced online, of elaborately decorated, themed reading areas. They spoke to the children's parents to gather specific information about the types of books and topics that each child particularly engaged with. Based on their engagement with literature around the development of early reading and their ongoing discussions about the development of their book area, they realised that their original question had focussed solely on one area of the provision and that they wanted to expand their research to think more broadly about how print media was utilised throughout the environment. Despite being quite far into their action research project, they decided that their investigations had led them to want to revise their research question to be "*how can we develop the environment to enable children to engage with reading?*" They had felt, through their discussions and research activity, that focussing solely upon the book area was missing opportunities to think about how book/texts were used in all areas of the provision. Their original research question had been a reflection of their thinking at the time that they created it. As their discussions and investigations developed their views, their question, consequently, also developed.

Planning and implementing a change

The planning stage of any action research cycle is the one that most people assume is the most important and they focus their energies on it. We are not arguing for downgrading its importance, rather it should be seen as part of a cyclical process where all stages matter, and omitting or skipping an aspect of the cycle can undermine the final value and outcomes from the project. This is why the planning for change stage also involves further reflection and information gathering, but of a much focussed sort. For example, if you wanted to develop the quality of oral language, having first established that it was a suitable focus, you might need to develop your own subject knowledge. This might include knowledge about the stages in oral language development, resources available, interventions, previous research into approaches for developing oral language, training opportunities, audits to assess practice and progress, and potential assessments that would support your evaluation of the project. Whilst every action research project is unique through the individuals and context involved, many of the foci are universal concerns and it is likely that there will be current research available outlining other people's approaches. This does not mean that you should copy what they do. Each setting is unique and the cherry-picking approach to educational reform of taking something that works in one place and dropping it into another context without mediation and support is discredited in practice (Winstanley, 2012). However, there are, potentially, lessons and resources that can save you time and heartache which might be usefully adapted with careful planning and thoughtful mediation.

Example from practice 1:

This is an account from a teacher about her project in Unicorn class for 4, 5, and 6 years old children with autism.

"When I started and joined the action research group, I didn't really know what I was going to do. All I knew was that I wanted to build something into our daily timetable which would be motivating and fun to develop the co-ordination needed for writing. It needed to be something that would help them improve their grip strength for holding a pencil and their position for holding a pencil. My research question became 'How might the introduction of different resources influence the pencil grip and strength and position in early writing?' We already recognise the need for activities that support gross and fine motor development, for example: Cbeebies Boogie Beebies dance; the Beam programme; Horse riding for gross motor development; Clever fingers activities are out every day, we have a lot of messy play, a lot of sensory play. Colleagues suggested a playdough disco. So, I went away and looked up various ones, some on the internet, some with crazy ladies, because quite a lot of the activities we do in class are whiteboard based because it really engages the children. But I thought about it and decided we couldn't do that and instead I came across this

(continued)

book by Alistair Bryce-Clegg (2011) 'Getting ready to Write' and that really fits the ethos of our classroom as we were already doing many of the activities suggested. But I had never analysed which upper body pivots or pencil grip positions the children were using to mark make previously. Following advice, I did this analysis and I decided on our own playdough disco as an intervention with the aim of improving fine motor movements, strength and co-ordination. The range of movements that can be incorporated into dough disco was a huge selling point for me. I could put in different exercises to address the needs of my cross-phase group from large-scale exercises focussing on the shoulder and elbow pivots, crossing the mid line to smaller fine motor control exercises such as isolating individual finger joints to develop the pincer grasp or strength to push and play that dough like a piano. It was a really good intervention for us. I spent a while researching what piece of music we could use for our disco and we ended up with a Minions version of Uptown Funk. I was going to change the music each week, but they love it so much that they expect it and we do it to that every day. We put dough disco into our timetable at the end of English each day. Each child had a lump of playdough as big as their heads. The children loved copying my crazy moves to the music. I looked at the different pencil grips the children had at the start and some of their writing samples. What actually happened was that everyone (children and adults) in the class was more focussed on pencil grips and trying to get children's writing positions that helped. But through doing the exercises e.g. pinch, pull and stretch the play dough, and doing big improvements such as swim, and cross the mid line. These were things not in the book, but we added them because we know the children and what they need.

The project has evolved as we have gone along. The children love it and they look forward to it, it has become a motivator. It gets some of them that find it hard to sit and listen to a whole story to keep going to get to the play dough disco.

It has worked really well. It has had a massive impact on their pencil grip. We took photographs of pencil grips before and after the intervention to track changes. So, this girl went from the palm super nova grip all the way through to static tripod grip. And these two boys have gone onto a full triangulation grip which is great. With the play dough disco they don't realise they are doing anything to do with strengthening their muscles, they just love it. We will carry on with the project and put more resources so they can have things they can hold, sticks, pencils and threading. They are quite happy to put the play dough down and do some of the bigger motion exercises. There is a lot more we could do with it looking to the future" (Joanne Dove).

The example above highlights the stages of the project. From having a general theme – "I wanted to do something about grip" through to asking a carefully formulated research question – "How might the introduction of different resources influence pencil grip strength and position in early writing?" This was backed up by data on the children's current pencil grip and position with observations and writing samples so that any progress could be tracked. The account highlights problems with using the internet, some content is unsuitable and deciding on what is credible and underpinned by educational research, and evidence informed can be challenging. It is important to have in mind the difference you want to make and to have some ideas of what that will look like at the end. In this case, there are clear diagrams and information on what the stages of pencil-grip development look like. How to move from the current situation to the end goal requires planning and innovation, which can take different forms. In the example from practice 1, it was a combination of ideas from colleagues, research, published materials, and practitioner knowledge and understanding of child development relating to early writing.

Innovate

Engagement with literature is important throughout the action research cycle to enable you, individually or as a team, to consider wider perspectives on the aspect of practice/provision that you are aiming to develop. However, at this planning stage, it is particularly important to be accessing information to support the development of ideas. Critically considering how other research or views interconnect with your own intentions, and the wider priorities for your setting, will enable you to consciously construct the rationale for the changes that you plan to implement. When we discuss literature, we mean evidence-informed research such as peer-reviewed academic articles and books by credible authorities in the sector. These need not be off-putting as often there are accessible versions in text books or educational magazines and specialist newspapers which often pick up academic works and provide overviews and summaries of the key points. But learning how to read research is an important skill as it can save you time and effort that might be otherwise wasted on ideas that are unsuitable. Abstracts are a good way into such papers as they provide a short summary of the whole article, including the findings. A quick scan can help you to see if the participants are similar to your setting, if the findings are positive and the ideas helpful. An alternative source is the wider internet and general newspapers. These are often referred to as "grey literature," and it is important to think carefully about the author and purpose of the article when you read them to make sure you are gaining the information you need and not just being "sold" something or misled. Keeping up to date with the latest developments in research can be helpful and many schools and settings have subscriptions to helpful sources. All of these sources, alongside ideas from colleagues can contribute to innovative ideas that inform the changes you implement to create the difference you want to make.

Example from practice 1 ...

Storytelling is an important area of early years practice, and one setting asked: "How can we develop independent storytelling in the early years?" They planned and

(continued)

implemented the following: a storytelling chair available in all foundations stage classes, a storytelling resource pack for each class with resource cards, a storytelling resource pack for outdoor areas, encouraged children to make up and tell their own stories, modelled storytelling language, engaged parents with storytelling activities to do at home, introduced special storytelling sessions into the routine, introduced props and resources to support independent storytelling, and used observations and recordings of children telling stories before and after to evaluate impact.

Example from practice 2 ...

A nursery class was keen to develop speaking and listening. They asked the question: How can the outside area be enhanced to provide high-quality opportunities to develop children's speaking and listening skills? They used observations to collect initial data that backed up their hypothesis that children were playing alongside each other but not communicating. They audited their outdoor area and provision and although it was satisfactory, decided that the outdoor area needed a revamp so they recruited a team of volunteers who worked over the Spring break. They created a mud kitchen and a gardening area where children would have to make decisions about what to grow, be responsible and run the space giving them purpose and audience for speaking and listening. A music area was created with a variety of props and a stage area to encourage interactions. A storytelling area was introduced in a special speaking and listening zone with a puppet theatre and a physical development area with a trolley of resources was made available. Alongside the zones and areas, mark making resources were always available helping children to think about communication in different ways. The ideas included children's suggestions about what would make the outside more engaging as well as practitioner suggestions.

Example from practice 3 ...

One setting was keen to develop early maths. They asked the question: "How can outdoor provision be improved to engage children in practical addition?" and developed the plan below:

- We got together as team and shared the research question

- We all thought of some ideas and activities (*They used internet sites to look up creative maths activities posted by teachers and academics, they read articles on early maths, maths text books, and attended a training session by an expert on creative early maths.*)

(continued)

■ Guide the learning rather than dominate. (*They used observations of children's interests to inform their planning.*)

■ More "maths" games (*e.g. the "addition machine", the "car ramp", doubling, dice, beads*).

■ As a team we wanted to think about asking deeper questions and recognising when to support children's spontaneous learning. For example, just because they aren't with number lines doesn't mean it isn't maths!

■ We asked children: What would happen if … and gave time for response.

■ Not just putting out maths resources for children to explore but key learning provided by staff through interactions.
  ● Really important for adults to be mathematical role models, modelling the correct use of language (*What do you think is happening? I wonder how many …? I don't know, what do you think? Tell me more about* … based on Sustained Shared Thinking (SST) Siraj-Blatchford, 2009).

From the plan they introduced a range of new number activities based on the suggestions above as well as helping practitioners to ask the questions and engage with children in ways that fostered deeper levels of understanding and modelled mathematical language and thinking. The session planning was altered to reflect more of a child interest focus.

Planning your implementation also means thinking about a range of other factors:

■ Who will be involved – all children or just one room group or class? A selection of children within a room, e.g. summer-born boys. Will all staff be invited to participate? What about parents or visitors? Remember, that excluding children from a focus group is problematic, and most practitioners find that they start with a small group in mind and the project expands because all children and staff want to be involved in an exciting and fun opportunity.

■ How long will the project run? A term, a year, longer? Remember that projects should go through at least full two cycles to be action research although often this can happen quite quickly. Many projects in this book initially began as projects for an academic year, approximately nine months and excluded holiday periods. Many were so successful they became part of the routine and practice or were extended into the following year. Some projects where much shorter such as the play dough disco project which was only planned for two terms, but was so successful that it was expanded into the next year and embedded into practice.

■ Are there budget or resource implications?

■ Do routines or staffing need to be adjusted or considered in some way? Are there other people not directly involved that need to be consulted?

- Do you need further parental or child consents to use data previously collected for another purpose or to gain additional data or access? (See ethics section in Part one).

- When will it end and how will you celebrate your work and share your findings? This could be at a dissemination event where you invite everyone involved to presentations on the project, maybe a display of children's work or photographs showing change over time. Some settings invite parents, governors, and children to share the celebration of trying something new, reflecting, and making changes that benefit children. It can be as informal or formal as you like, but it is usually a nice idea to recognise and share your work.

- How will you evaluate its impact or outcomes? This is a key question and one that should be built into the plan from the very beginning and often starts with the initial data collection to confirm the current situation.

All of these considerations will impact on the final shape of your project. We provide a proforma (Appendix IV) that can be used to support this planning phase of your project.

> **Example from practice: Dissemination event**
>
> One setting organises an annual celebration and dissemination event at their local town hall. They take a gallery space for a short time and display work by the children to showcase the learning over that year. Parents, governors, children, and the local community are invited, and the display is open for anyone in the local area to drop in and view over a week. They also invite other settings that they have worked within a facilitated action research network to participate. The displays include specific posters about the various action research projects undertaken by the settings. The posters show the cycle of action research from identifying a focus, formulating a research question, collating information, planning and implementing a change, the all-important critical reflection throughout, and the evaluation of impact and planning for the future. Each poster is different as they highlight the different projects and the individual approaches taken, although the cycle is similar. Examples of children's work, photographs, and before and after data highlight any impact and progress made.

Evaluating Impact

Making a difference is often a rationale identified by practitioners for engaging with action research. Identifying what that difference might be and how it might be evaluated are important aspects of the action research cycle. In the model we propose, an impact evaluation framework is suggested (see Appendix III) and explained here.

How will you know you have been successful?

The framework starts by asking you to imagine the children after a successful project. What will you see, hear, and observe in the children as a result of your work? For example, practitioners often say the children will be more confident. But that is vague; you need to articulate what "confident" would look like or sound like for that particular group of children in that specific context. What kind of language or interactions might characterise the imagined confident child? Trying to be specific as possible is helpful at this stage as it provides a clear vision of the end goal. Imagining and articulating that difference enables practitioners to create a type of success criteria for the outcomes from their project. Some outcomes might be measurable using standard setting data such as Foundation Stage profiles or checklists associated with aspects of development or audits of provision and its usage or popularity with children. Other outcomes, and these are usually the ones most valued by practitioners, are less easily measured such as dispositions and attitudes, quality of interactions, motivation, and engagement. Having a clear idea and ideally some ways of identifying this change in mind at the beginning of the project makes it much easier to then revisit and to evaluate both at regular stages throughout and at the end of the project. A helpful way of thinking about impact is to return to the original impact evaluation developed by Earley and Porritt that suggested thinking about it in three ways: as products, processes, and impact/outcomes. Products are often easier to consider as these are usually some sort of artefact, for example in Part three of this book, Aberdeen Park created a new Continuing Professional Development (CPD) policy. Processes or systems might also be interpreted as alternative teaching approaches such as dough disco. But the impact/outcome is the key, and this is evidenced by how the product/s and process/es make a difference to the learning and experiences of practitioners and children (Earley & Porritt, 2010:8). In the example of dough disco it is the change in attitude and behaviours of children leading to improved pencil grip as a result of a change to routine and the introduction of resources and an intervention.

Example from practice 1 ...

Lauren and Karen were interested in finding out whether immersing children in storytelling language would improve their writing. They wanted the difference to be that all children would be confident storytellers. They imagined that after a successful project, the children would be keen to tell stories, there would be a "buzz" about storytelling and that this enthusiasm would feed into writing stories.

They used observations to evaluate current practice and to create a baseline against which to evaluate the project. This enabled them to articulate more fully what confident storytelling, motivation to engage with storytelling, and "buzz" around storytelling might look like.

(continued)

They were able to evaluate their project using before and after samples of children's writing, before and after observations of child-initiated storytelling. They collected children's views before and after and data for speaking and listening. In evaluating their project, they were able to compare the "before and after" and reflect on their own practice and any changes.

Example from practice 2 …

Nicola was interested in finding the most effective strategies to help a group of children manage/express their emotions. She identified two children who appeared to have challenges in managing or expressing emotions. Nicola used observations and a Boxall profile of each child before and after to evaluate her project. The difference she wanted to make was a reduction in emotional outbursts per week, leading to a higher level of emotional well-being for each child.

Example from practice 3 …

Developing the outdoor area is a popular focus for action research projects. It can be an expensive and longer time-frame topic. One setting wanted to develop their outdoor area, and this was identified as part of a larger upgrade of the environment. As a result, although they made a plan, they had to wait for fund-raising followed by large-scale earth works. They responded by planning a two-part project made up of two cycles of the action research process. Part 1 was what they could do whilst the earth works were in progress. They involved the children and used the experience as a learning opportunity as well as investigating and planning for the next cycle. In the second cycle, they had already influenced the larger-scale works and had a very clear plan for the implementation for how the new spaces would be used. Their ultimate product was an improved outdoor area, the processes in achieving this developed team work, children's voice, and community support for the setting. The impact/outcome was a positive and happy environment, behaviours were improved, and children were stimulated and engaged with improved outdoor learning.

Evaluating the impact is not just about the development of the aspect of provision under scrutiny. As discussed previously, the action research process is as much about the development of teams and individuals as it is about developing practice. Earley and Porritt (2010) considered differing approaches to CPD within education and outline the importance of impact evaluation that is embedded into the design of professional development activity. Planning for, and maintaining, reflective evaluation of the impact of your action research upon your own, and the team's, development, is an integral feature of the action research cycle. Capturing and recording the project as it progresses is helpful and writing reflective journals can often assist in reviewing and reflecting upon developing ideas and recording moments, thoughts, and key questions.

Example from practice-reflective journals

A group of early years teams from the London Borough of Islington participated in a facilitated action research project. As part of the project, they were given high-quality A4 scrapbooks to serve as reflective journals. The idea was to use them to capture the input from the facilitated sessions, but also their ideas, questions, worries, and thoughts about the project as it progressed. The books were personal and private to individuals, although many found it helpful to use them as workbooks for ideas about planning and implementing, sticking in articles or pictures, and lists of resources or thoughts which they shared and discussed at their regular project meetings. They valued having the books as it created an ongoing record of their work and became a resource they used both for the project and beyond. It also captured their personal professional learning as they participated in the action research cycles. "The journal was a good thing, a record of a really interesting journey" (Elisabet Epinosa).

Considering the future

The cyclical process of action research can often mean that there is no specific end point. The completion of one cycle might merely establish further questions for continued scrutiny. Whilst this may seem unhelpfully vague, it is important to reflect upon both the past and the future to consider both what you have learned throughout the process and what questions have emerged that may require further investigation. The pro forma (Appendix VI) may be useful in structuring this reflection, to support you to consider what you have learned, what influence the process has had upon your provision, what questions you have been left with, and, importantly, what you are going to do about them.

A further consideration is the dissemination of your research. Sharing the process as well as the outcomes enables other practitioners to consider the congruence or incongruence to their own context, and consequently the relevance of your investigations for practice within their own setting. Opening a dialogue with other practitioners and settings may add valuable insights to the direction of your own practice or contribute to new avenues for investigations.

Irrespective of the new directions that you head towards during this phase of the process, it is important that you maintain oversight of the aspect of practice that you have been researching and the ongoing consequences of the changes that you have implemented. It is important to recognise that "impact" from research activity is not necessarily immediately obvious. Maintaining focus on the issue that has formed the focus of the research will enable further, longer term, consequences to be identified and reflected upon. It is highly likely that ongoing ripples from your research activity will cause impact, both on you/your team and the provision well into the future.

Example from practice 1 ...

One school-based EYFS setting had been focussing on developing their environment to support children's engagement in outdoor learning activities. Having incorporated "child's voice" into their research, to support them to consider the way in which the outdoor learning environment was constructed, they had recognised the need for children to feel that they had some ownership of the space and realised the value in children being able to share their views. This proved to be a significant realisation for the setting and, following the action research project, they are committed to ensuring that the children's views were sought more frequently in wider decision-making processes. This commitment resulted in the whole school giving consideration to the opportunities that were provided for children to voice their views on aspects of school life.

Example from practice 2 ...

One room leader in an EYFS setting had initially wanted to focus on ways to develop the setting's parent partnerships. After discussions with other staff members, she decided to start with a small-scale action research investigation into the key-worker role within her room (1- to 2-year-olds). She used a questionnaire to explore parent's views on the current communication processes, and to gather perspectives on ways in which the parents would like to share information about their child with the key workers. Through the questionnaires, as well as discussions with parents and staff, she became increasingly aware that some parents were feeling excluded from information sharing, as they were not often present at key times in the day (drop-off and pick-up times). From this, the room leader began to develop alternative channels for two-way communication, including utilising the platform from the e-learning journals, developing the use of communication books, designating time for telephone discussions, and developing a pro forma for celebrating children's significant achievements. In evaluating the consequences of the changes to these practices, the room leader and staff felt that it had enhanced the quality and frequency of the interactions between parents and key workers. Subsequently, other room leaders within the setting were inspired to focus upon strengthening the relationships between parents and key workers, some utilising some of the practices developed through the 1- to 2-year-old's room leader's action research. In addition, the room leader decided to develop the documentation used to support children's introduction to the nursery, to include specific discussion about preferred methods of communication from the outset, so that new parents to the setting would be able to express preferences and develop communication channels that best suited their individual situations.

It is also important to keep up the momentum in dialogue/reflection within teams. Practitioners often note the significance of the collaborations within teams and, if this has proved beneficial, there is no need to restrict collaboration to specified research projects. If interpersonal dynamics have benefitted from the action research process, then recognising these and, maintaining them, can be very valuable.

Example from practice 3 ...

One feature of the Facilitated Action Research in the Early Years projects has been the collaboration between EYFS settings. Different settings participating in action research activity specifically relevant to their own context, share their research, periodically, throughout the process and discuss their individual aspects of practice. This has been highlighted by participants as a particularly beneficial facet, as professional dialogue enables practitioners, at all levels, to contemplate how common practices are enacted differently in different contexts. This enables practitioners to consider challenges in new ways or deepen understanding of the differing contextual features of different settings. It has also led to practitioners implementing changes to practices within their own settings, in response to the action research activity undertaken by others, or to resolve to investigate an aspect of practice more deeply, within their own setting, in response to an aspect researched by others in theirs.

Summary

The action research cycle that we present identifies specific phases for guiding you through the process. Each phase requires cycles of planning, acting, observing, and reflecting in order to develop the depth of understanding necessary to take the research project forward. The initial phase encourages action researchers to consider the challenges that you encounter within your practice and begin to envisage an alternative scenario. This phase also encourages you to contemplate the factors that are motivating current practice and identify aspects which require further scrutiny. This then should lead you towards an initial research question which stems from a genuine interest in developing your understanding and exploring avenues for adaptation and change.

The second phase of our cycle involves collecting information to explore the current situation further and consider the particular area of focus in greater detail. This requires continued critical reflection in order to question some of the assumptions which may have emerged from your initial identification phase. The information that you collect will be wholly dependent upon your individual area of focus and your individual context, but it should always be gathered with conscious consideration of ethical practices and ethical use of the data. The information collated at this phase can also act as a useful benchmark for facilitating the evaluation of the impact of your research activity later in the cycle.

The third phase, planning and implementing a change, requires careful consideration of the information collected and reflection upon the initial research question. Having identified an area for focus and explored it in greater depth, the changes to be planned should be identified in response to your ongoing and developing views of the difference that you would like to see. The intentions for evaluating the consequences of your changes will be dependent upon your individual choices and your individual context, however, some thought should be given to continually reviewing impact and adapting in response to potential trajectories.

The fourth phase, evaluating impact, requires that you give thought to the difference that you have made, the contributory factors, and the influence of the changes that you introduced. The data collected during phase two can act as an important asset in forming these judgements and determining future directions.

The fifth phase, considering the future, requires you to look ahead to where you might go next. For some, this might mean starting a new action research cycle in response to new questions or new challenges. For others it might mean identifying some longer term changes in response to your explorations. Disseminating your research activity is also an important element of this phase. Sharing your process and your views on the impact of your research can be very beneficial, particularly if undertaking action research as an individual. Continuous reflection upon the influence of your action research upon you, as a practitioner, is important throughout. However, it is often during this fifth stage when the real impact of the process is recognisable. This can often be due to opening up to broader questions and recognition of the complexities of practice in the EYFS. Research is often much more about finding questions than it is about finding answers.

Part three
The projects

Introduction

This chapter provides detailed examples of ten action research projects carried out by early years practitioners in settings across London and the Southeast. Each follows the phases outlined within Part two and provides an account of the impact upon the setting, the children, and the practitioners' professional development. The projects cover the complete early years age range from baby room to infant classes. They reflect the depth and breadth of issues facing practitioners from curriculum to environment, and from practice to policy. It might have been nice to have a project for every area of the early years curriculum or from each possible age-range combination. But things falling neatly into predefined categories is not the reality of early years practice. Instead, the projects reflect the complexity of practice and the balancing of needs, priorities, and resources that practitioners face every day in their settings. The focus of projects chosen by practitioners made sense to them within their contexts. But this means that there might be some projects where you as a reader wonder "how did they come to choose that focus?" In presenting the projects we hope to show that the topic and scope is less important than the engagement with reflection, action research cycles, and a desire to make a difference through addressing an issue of personal and professional interest to those involved.

Ten projects: Each project is presented in the same format and sequence. All the projects begin with the project title, followed by the issue leading to a focussed question. A narrative overview of the project is provided by depicting the cyclical processes and adopting the format from Part two (Identifying a focus, Collating information, Planning and implementing a change, Evaluating impact, and Considering the future). The projects are supported by photographs, reflections, and commentaries by practitioners on what they learnt, what the difference was, and their thoughts looking ahead.

It is important to note that each project was chosen by practitioners in response to a particular issue or question that they themselves identified within their context at that particular moment in time. Therefore, each project is a personal reflection of those practitioners and their understanding and context when the project began. It is not in any way a list of projects you should try in your setting. Instead, each project acts as an illustration of the process that all projects go through when undertaking action research. We intend that the stages and principles underpinning the projects should be taken on board and applied to the focus that matters to you and your setting.

Mindful yoga in a nursery school

This first project is deliberately positioned as an example of a project that perhaps challenges some preconceived ideas about what a typical action research project in an early years environment might focus on and look like. We chose to place this first to highlight our view that projects should reflect the individual interest and contexts and are not necessarily linked to national priorities or curricula areas. Indeed, some of the best projects are creative and innovative ideas that challenge the status quo and offer alternatives to established views about "this is what we do and this is how we do it" which can be easy to adopt in the face of conflicting agenda from policy, practice, and stakeholders internally and externally. We hope that this project will support practitioners in thinking differently about what might constitute a suitable area for enquiry and using a combination of personal and professional insights and interests to create a project that has a positive impact on children.

Yoga is featured on the Education Endowment toolkit as an intervention which may have some benefits at relatively low cost for early years. It is a focus that attracts interest as it offers insights into children's self-regulation and inhibitory control, which are functionally related to emotional regulation and executive functions (EFs) and therefore are of great interest in early years.

EFs develop to help children in ignoring unnecessary distractions in order to accomplish a goal (Diamond & Lee, 2011). In mindful yoga, children are required to focus on particular poses and learn how to regulate their breath, their bodies, and their minds, which mirrors the processes of EF. Yoga as an activity has research support as a way to improve EFs of young children and is easy to incorporate into school curricula (Diamond & Lee, 2011). The argument suggests that if children are regulated emotionally, they can better focus at school and perform better with a variety of benefits for children beyond simply doing better at school; being able to control one's emotions leads to healthier relationships, decreased likelihood of incarceration, and better mental health (Macklem, 2008). The mindfulness practices involved in yoga for children such as breathing, meditations, and bodily control have all been used in research studies as ways to teach children how to control their emotions. Mindfulness has been studied in adults as a preventative measure and therapeutic intervention for anxiety and depression, and research was hopeful for the effects on children as well. A study by Razza, Bergen-Cico, and Raymond et al. (2013) used mindful yoga as a way to enhance young children's self-regulation, and self-regulation is functionally related to emotional regulation. As this project was undertaken by an early years practitioner who was also a qualified yoga instructor, there was a personal incentive in exploring yoga and executive function to improve teaching and to help others in their endeavours to incorporate yoga into their curricula.

Understanding the mechanisms behind the behaviours and emotions that children express led to a desire to implement a practice which could help children cope better in emotionally charged situations. There were no studies focusing specifically on yoga for emotional regulation in children.

Project summary

This project was undertaken as part of a Masters level dissertation by a practitioner who was also a qualified yoga instructor. Research suggests yoga might help with self-regulation and inhibitory control, which are functionally related to emotional regulation. The research purpose was to understand how yoga influenced the way children perceived and controlled their emotions in order to provide educators and yoga instructors with the insight that could influence their daily practice. The research was intended to benefit the participants, and to help them understand their own emotions better. It was decided that the link between EF and mindful yoga should be the focus of this study, with a particular focus on emotional regulation.

1. Identifying a focus

Research highlighted the mindfulness practices involved in yoga for children, such as breathing, meditations, and bodily control. All these practices have been used as ways to teach children how to control their emotions. Mindfulness has been studied in adults as a preventative measure and therapeutic intervention for anxiety and depression. The project aimed to study these effects on children and whether yoga could be legitimised as an intervention for children who struggle to control their emotions?

2. Collating information

First, I had to gather information about executive functions and how emotional regulation is developed in young children. Initial emotional-regulation ability was measured through a baseline questionnaire which was completed by the children's teacher. Interviews were also conducted to better understand how the focus children were understanding their emotions and their ability to control these emotions.

3. Planning and implementing a change

The project explored how mindful yoga could be adapted to specifically target emotional-regulation skills. Each lesson plan was designed based on the feedback from the previous session through self-reflection journals. The sessions were constantly adapted to the children and the skills they were excelling in and needed help with. This was both to help the children with emotional regulation and also to better improve the mindful yoga practice itself. The six children in the study were asked to participate in 11 in-school sessions of mindful yoga, which combined elements of physical practice and mindfulness exercises. A typical session lasted 40 minutes, with the children playing various yoga games, practising breathing techniques, and engaging in guided relaxation time. The children in the study attended the sessions in lieu of their free-flow activity time twice a week, and observations were conducted after the sessions to note the progress of two focus children, one with high emotional-regulation ability and one with low emotional-regulation ability.

Cycle diagram: Identify a focus → Collate information → Plan and implement a change → Evaluate impact → Consider the future

5. Considering the future

There is a need for inexpensive, effective, and accessible interventions for the development of children's executive functioning. Once taught, yoga can be applied in a setting on a regular basis, whether used throughout the day or as a dedicated time of the routine. Children found that yoga gave them specific tools such as breathing and physical control. These practices would be useful for teachers to incorporate into transition times or through taking breaks in between lessons. The lessons can be to meet children's individual needs demonstrating that yoga is a flexible practice which can be adapted for children of all learning styles and abilities. Other interventions shown to aid in children's executive functioning, such as computer programs or traditional martial arts, are much more complicated and rigorous in terms of training practitioners to be able to carry out these interventions, supporting the view that yoga is a cost-effective, beneficial, and easy approach to adopt as a way to aid in children's functioning and potentially provide practitioners with an accessible way to incorporate executive functioning training into children's everyday routines.

4. Evaluating impact

The results indicated that the children learned practices which they could use at home or throughout the school day in order to calm themselves down. They also gained internal awareness and physical control which led to better emotional control. This emotional control was thought to be a reason for the increase in academic performance found at the end of the study.

2 Developing the outdoor area to support early numeracy

This project was carried out at a four-form entry infant school in Kent. The vision for this school is "To create independent, happy, healthy and confident people by developing their skills for lifelong learning in an ever changing world". The school heard about a Facilitated Action Research programme run by tutors from a university and held at a local nursery school as after-school hours twilight sessions from the local head teacher network. As a school, they decided this would be a good professional development opportunity and participated. They signed up for the programme and attended an information, introduction session at the end of the autumn term, participating in three further sessions spread over the spring term, and culminating in a celebration and dissemination event in the summer term linked to Foundation Profile moderation. The focus on learning provided by action research chimed with the school ethos and statement which outlines their approach to learning:

> At Shears Green Infant School we are focussed on enabling children to become confident and creative builders of their own future. We do this through a team of people who are caring, nurturing and supportive to each individual. We promote and continuously develop a creative curriculum with purpose and meaning to the lives of the children we serve. The curriculum encompasses the richness of the children's lives, the local community and the evolving world around them. We believe children can meet the academic challenges we present to them with openness, enthusiasm and willingness to solve problems. We believe in creating an environment where appropriate risks can be taken creating socially and academically responsible people. Through providing a school climate whereby children feel happy, safe and supported we believe we will provide lifelong learners to the world.
>
> (Sheers Green Infant School)

The school's focus on empowerment fits with a professional development opportunity provided by facilitated action research that supports practitioners to learn how to carry out a project supported by tutors and to move through the stages so that they can continue to address issues and questions about practice through future action research projects. Shears Green Infant School adopted this approach and took part in two facilitated projects and then felt empowered and confident to undertake projects independently. The project outlined in this section reflects an early project and the leaflet and presentation they created as part of the dissemination event at the end of the academic year.

Project summary

Shears Green Infant School looked at their Foundation Stage Profile data and school development plan. These indicated that maths was an area for potential development. At a local head teacher network, meeting the opportunity for participating in a Facilitated Action Research project was offered by the Early Foundations Teaching School Alliance. School heads suggested that a focus on developing outdoor areas might be useful or a focus on specific curriculum area in response to school development plans and data. At Shears Green Infant School, teachers identified children's engagement in child-initiated activities with the focus on maths as an area to explore. This project was the outcome of that initial discussion and is presented in the words of those involved.

5. Considering the future

The use of mathematical language by children in telling us what they liked reflects the learning. The project has been a success in that we have increased the range and type of resources as well as their availability inside and outside. The children have greater opportunities to explore independently and to engage in child-initiated maths activities. They choose to follow up the adult-directed activities and are more motivated to try things. The increase in resources and the project have changed the way we set up the outdoor environment, and this is now part of our routine and practice. Looking ahead, we will continue to monitor and develop all aspects of maths through independent learning in child-initiated activities both inside and outside. Through the development of the outside area, we will ensure there is a good range of mathematical problem-solving practical activities available to enable all children to access and achieve.

4. Evaluating impact

Although we saw an improvement in the data when we introduced this strategy, we found there were still children who were not accessing the maths resources either due to own choice or weather. To tackle this, we introduced "inside challenges". This has allowed all the children to access extra maths resources whether they are inside or outside in child-initiated time. We asked the children about the changes we have made: "I like the number bonds to 10 song", "I liked matching the eggs to the dinosaurs", and "I liked it when we had to do sphere and cylinder and all those". Data showed a good level of progress towards children achieving Early Learning Goals in number and calculation. Pupil voice shows that children enjoy number work and have a better understanding of the application of number.

(Diagram: cycle of — Identify a focus → Collate information → Plan and implement a change → Evaluate impact → Consider the future)

1. Identifying a focus

We held year group meetings to look at current provision and to consider what could be altered to improve the confidence of the cohort when applying number to their play. Observations about perceived lower levels of engagement by children in child-initiated maths activities outdoors, coupled with Foundation stage profile data suggested this was an area for development. It led to thinking about how to increase the opportunities for children to access maths learning during child initiated/independent/outside activities. This was turned into a focussed research question asking: How can outdoor provision be improved to engage children through child-initiated activities in the application of calculation?

2. Collating information

We looked at current data and identified areas for improvement. Observations and children's learning journals were used to reflect on the maths activities children had been engaged with, and to identify children not engaging. From this, individuals were identified who were not engaging in maths activities during child-initiated time, and they became the target group, although the project was for all children in the cohort.

3. Planning and implementing a change

Our expectations were that children would tackle problems, use mathematical vocabulary, and be resilient when solving problems to get an answer. In response to our focus, we planned to boost the maths opportunities children have to access maths in our outdoor area. This involved increasing the maths resources outside that children could access. We have weekly maths challenges during small group time. These are left out for the children in child-initiated time so they can access and explore them independently. It was helpful to have some specialist subject input on mathematical activities and learning opportunities that we could adapt and adopt for ourselves and our setting. All adults were given information grids for focus children where interaction with the challenges would be beneficial. At the beginning of each child-initiated session, the children are informed of the challenges and given the tools to achieve the challenge.

3 Storytelling

Storytelling is a popular focus in early years due to its importance in supporting children's oral language development and early writing. Oral language is key for enabling children to rehearse their thinking and support their understanding and is crucial in developing social relationships and communication skills. As a prime area in the Foundation Stage, this importance is recognised and highlighted for children and practitioners. Research recognises the challenges for practitioners with increasing numbers of children arriving in nursery and schools with seemingly low levels of oral language and its impact on their development (Norbury et al., 2016). A range of potential factors that may contribute to this from increasing levels of English as an additional language to developmental delay, increased use of technology leading to reduced interactions, changes in parenting interactions, and issues around socio-economic status are often proposed (Whorrall & Cabell, 2016). However, perhaps more important in our view is what practitioners might be able to do to mitigate the effects of low levels of oral language and the lack of development in speaking and listening.

Action research offers an opportunity to focus on developing oral language through a range of creative and innovative approaches to suit the needs of the children and context. Several nurseries and schools chose to focus on developing oral language for their action research projects which meant a difficult decision about which specific project to use as an example of a complete project. To recognise the excellent work by all the oral language projects we have drawn upon several as part of the examples produced elsewhere in the text and chosen to use a project from Blean Primary School which adopted the "Helicopter Story" intervention approach. This approach is well documented and researched (Cremin et.al., 2017) and a popular approach adopted by many settings as an intervention to support oral language. The project also utilised the *Record of Oral Language* (Clay et al., 1983). Rachel from Blean outlines her rationale for the project below, and the project is detailed on the following pages.

> My setting was drawn to a focus "Communication and Language" because of our knowledge of the children, data trends over time and our recognition of the importance of responding to the changing demographic of our local community. For the last three years the number of pupils for whom EAL has increased to nearly a third of each Early Years Foundation Stage class, and our Language and Speech Link assessments are no longer enough to elicit exactly how we can support these pupils.

Project summary

Although storytelling is a key part of the provision and routine, observations and data alongside a sense that it wasn't working as well as it could led to a decision to focus on storytelling specifically within the wider area of communication and language. A creative approach was needed, and engagement in a facilitated action research project enabled Rachel and her colleagues to focus on the issue. By investigating possible options, current practice, and literature available they created a successful project that made a difference to the children.

1. Identifying a focus

With an increase in children with English as an additional language to over a third of the cohort, existing provision was not sufficient to meet the needs of children. This led to Foundation Stage data and observations identifying development of oral language as a priority. The research question became, "how can we promote children's oral language through storytelling?"

2. Collating information

We already had observations and data and we heard and recorded the grammatical structures the children used, but the Record of Oral Language (Clay et al., 1983) assessment helped to refine and focus on what was age appropriate for those pupils and which gaps we needed to address. This assessment tool gave a numerical score for the children's use of oral language and the results surprised us – in what the children knew and didn't know and what we as practitioners knew and didn't know about early language development.

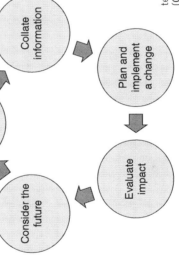

3. Planning and implementing a change

We had an extensive range of existing practice including using a "story whoosh", story sacks, shared reading, poems, and rhymes, but we were not really using oral storytelling. We used the results from the Record of Oral Language (Clay et al., 1983) assessment to fine-tune our modelling of grammatical language structures.

An approach that drew our interest involved promoting the children as authors, where we acted as scribes for the children and wrote down their special stories in books each adult carried in the setting. We implemented this easily – children were very curious about these books, watching their spoken words becoming print in front of their eyes, and quickly learnt to love and seek out these opportunities for us to scribe as they enjoyed performing and watching others perform these stories which we read aloud at the end of each session.

4. Evaluating impact

The statistical data was overwhelmingly positive and evident in the quantitative data the Record of Oral Language Assessment (Clay et al., 1983) provided. More so, our learning environments fizzled with children who would confidently tell the adults "I have a story to tell you" and wait for us to be ready to write every word down! The children paused for effect, checked we had recorded all of their ideas, and beamed proudly when they were recognised for "writing" that story we had just performed. It engaged all, as all the children enjoyed taking part in telling or acting out stories, and many children used old books from our stockroom to start scribing their own and others' stories.

5. Considering the future

This project gave us an opportunity to make a sustained difference to our provision, and seeing the impact so clearly in the setting has proven its worth in our future planning. We have decided as a team to further explore oral storytelling by engaging in Helicopter Story training, and we are keen to further develop our "author" approach with the children this year too. We will be including the use of the Record of Oral Language (Clay et al., 1983) assessment tool as part of our assessment schedule too.

Continuing professional development policy

Continuing professional development (CPD), also known as professional learning, is an important part of early years. But there may be a tendency for it to be dominated by compliance training rather than professional learning opportunities. For example, there are legal requirements for settings to meet regulatory criteria. Ofsted as the inspectorate and regulatory body has clear expectations about ensuring practitioners have current training and accreditation where appropriate in areas such as safeguarding, first aid, and food hygiene. We are not suggesting that these are not important, but rather that a balance needs to be struck between ensuring regulatory and safety compliance alongside other forms of professional development and learning. We argue that settings need to invest in building capacity within the staff team and providing opportunities for personal and professional development that is pedagogically and praxis orientated. The rationales are multiple but from a pragmatic position start with the challenges of recruiting and retaining suitable staff in the early years' sector. They are also firmly connected to debates about quality and parental choice with developing practitioners as a crucial part of ensuring improved outcomes for children. Engaging in action research can offer a potential solution to balancing the needs of children with those of practitioner learning and development within a tight budget and external pressures. In light of these challenges, there may be a tendency for practitioners to focus on children and their outcomes without necessarily considering how having motivated, engaged, and valued practitioners may impact upon children's outcomes and the quality of provision. In the next project, practitioners started thinking about children and wanted to undertake a project that would make a difference to practice. They began by identifying a specific early years' pedagogical approach, Sustained Shared Thinking, and then considering what they need to know and do to implement it. This led to a realisation that understanding their settings approach to continuing professional development opportunities would be beneficial before embarking on a child-centred project.

Project summary

This project is a great example of the changing foci caused by continuous reflection and refinement of ideas through practitioner collaboration. Initially starting as a focus on adult and child interactions within the setting, leading to consideration of staff training needs for developing interactions, the explorations and discussions illuminated bigger issues relating to staff development. The setting leaders and practitioners realised through the action research process that continuous professional development (CPD) opportunities offered to staff were not always giving the most consideration to individual staff needs. Through discussions, reflection, and questionnaires, the participating group realised that there was a need for a specific CPD policy within their setting to ensure that processes for staff development were unified and communicated clearly. The investigations, undertaken through the action research process, enabled the group to consider aspects of practice within the setting that had not been given particular scrutiny previously. This also enabled the setting leaders to reflect upon their own practices in leading aspects of provision.

5. Considering the future

Setting leaders presented their action research activity and outcomes to the setting's trustees. The group shared their action research project with other practitioners within the area and planned to explore further CPD opportunities to increase the offer available to staff. The group also recognised the need to maintain focus on the CPD policy to ensure that it continued to reflect the setting's procedures and suitably fulfil staff needs.

4. Evaluating impact

The group planned a further questionnaire to consider staff views again following the implementation of the new policy to evaluate the difference in practitioner perspectives on CPD. In addition, the group noted an increase in staff applying for CPD opportunities being offered, and a greater enthusiasm for reflecting upon their individual requirements, enquiring about available CPD and discussion about sharing their existing expertise in particular areas across the team.

1. Identifying a focus

The project started with a group of setting leaders and practitioners within an EYFS setting. After discussing the various aspects of practice that could become the focus of further investigation, it was decided that adult interaction and the development of Sustained Shared Thinking would be an area of interest. After initially exploring the CPD needs of practitioners to support them to consider their training requirements, the group broadened their focus to investigate staff development throughout the setting and reconsider how CPD opportunities were being determined and offered.

2. Collating information

The group decided to use staff questionnaires to explore practitioner perspectives. This allowed them to gain greater insight into views on CPD, practitioner understanding of CPD opportunities, views on the value of CPD being offered, and general views on individual's CPD requirements. This enabled the group to develop a clearer sense of practitioners' understanding and also highlighted some limitations in current practices for communicating about staff development within the setting. Continuous discussion amongst the group, and contemplation upon the collated information from the whole staff team, culminated in the decision to create a clear policy for CPD to be applied throughout the setting.

3. Planning and implementing a change

The development of a structured policy to communicate entitlement, outline processes, and unify procedures for identifying and organising CPD opportunities for the whole staff team became the planned change. This was to be developed by the group in continued discussion with the staff team as a whole.

5 Personal, social, and emotional development at lunchtime

Lunchtimes are often a potentially fraught period in schools and settings. The structure of the timetabled routine is often more relaxed, and midday meal supervisors (MDMS) rather than teachers and practitioners may take responsibility for the children during this period. Space, time, and people change the usual dynamics, and children can find the experience overwhelming.

The Oaks Infant School identified children's well-being at lunchtimes as an issue to explore. They wondered if the existing approach was working as well as it could to support children with the lunchtime experience. This interest in lunchtime and how it is managed to best support children echoes current research and foci on children's mental health; well-being; and personal, social, and emotional development (World Health Organisation, 2003).

This project is particularly interesting as it started in the early years and expanded to include the whole school. It also engaged a wider range of staff than the usual lead practitioners working on the project in their own classroom or setting room. Working with a wider team has both advantages and disadvantages for action research. As an individual it is easier to identify a focus that you are personally and professionally interested in for your own context. Including a range of colleagues requires a focus that all are equally interested and committed too or can find something within that engages them for the duration of the project. Linked to that is the discussion and exploration of the issue so that all feel equally involved, valued, and listened to in drawing up a plan and committing to a course of action.

In this project the deputy head teacher took the lead and this again has potential issues around power and equality. In most action research projects, the class teachers or room leads take responsibility for their personally interesting and professionally motivating projects. One of the most powerful aspects of action research is the ownership of projects by participants and how the projects speak to individuals and their own motivations, interests, and purpose leading to improvements for children. Fortunately, in this example the project focus was a popular choice and staff felt interested and engaged with the challenge of improving lunchtimes for the children, so any power issues around being directed by a more senior colleague did not occur, this was also due to the positive relationships and school ethos.

Project summary

This project was initially discussed as a project about well-being with a focus on making a positive difference to children's lunchtime experiences. It began with a particular focus on the younger children who might at times feel overwhelmed by the lunchtime experience. But very quickly the project expanded to include the whole school, as lunchtimes were a shared and common experience across all age groups and from staff observations and children's feedback identified as an area that could be improved. This project benefited from a school working party approach which meant that there was a behaviour steering group already in existence that could be involved in the project and advise.

5. Considering the future

Including MDMS in senior leadership meetings was a new approach, and looking ahead there is still work to be done on embedding this aspect and ensuring it remains helpful. MDMS also need to be consistently included in professional development opportunities. Next steps include working with year one to create an undercover area outside. The project appears to have been a success, but the next steps are about embedding the improved practices and ensuring that routine and consistency do not reduce the quality of the interactions and outcomes.

4. Evaluating impact

An unexpected but welcome outcome from this project was the empowerment of MDMS and others. They felt their voices were both listened to and acted upon, creating a determination to improve lunchtimes and consistency between staff. The project was evaluated against the success criteria set at the beginning of the project in terms of how children and adults were experiencing lunchtimes. An audit against the checklist interactions initially used for baseline data was repeated. Regular reporting through the checklist and meetings supported the evaluation and provided reflections for next steps. Improved well-being for children and reduced behavioural, social, and emotional issues at the beginning of the afternoon sessions suggest positive outcomes.

Identify a focus

Collate information

Consider the future

Plan and implement a change

Evaluate impact

1. Identifying a focus

The teacher and child experience of the beginning of the school afternoon leads to this focus. Both children and adults were finding the lunchtime period challenging leading to staff dealing with disputes and emotional issues from children before the afternoon learning could commence. These arose mainly due to social interactions and communication issues during the lunchtime period. The participants framed the difference they wanted to achieve from the project. They focussed on what the adults would be doing and saying and how that would lead to improved experiences for children. Considering the difference and articulating this clearly supported the development of success criteria for the project and its subsequent evaluation.

2. Collating information

Observations of lunchtime interactions and pupil voices provided an initial indicator of the lunchtime situation and child experience. Leuven scales were used to create an initial baseline for children's well-being. Assemblies were used as another opportunity to discuss lunchtimes with children, their current experiences and challenges, and what could be done.

3. Planning and implementing a change

A group of staff across a range of roles attended external training which provided an inspirational input on activities and approaches to managing the lunchtime period. Children and staff were consulted on what would make lunchtimes happier and the suggestions were incorporated into a plan. Children drew pictures and an adapted Mosaic approach (Clark, 2005) for collecting their views was adopted under the banner of "Make lunchtimes amazing!" From these a series of quick wins and longer term goals were drawn up. Key to the implementation was training for MDMS and discussion and clarity over roles and responsibilities. A MDMS self-assessment checklist was introduced, MDMS were included in the senior leadership meetings, and a rotational plan for lunchtime activities was implemented.

6 Talking Partners at Primary

Although this book is focussed on the early years, which in the English EYFS covers children aged 0–5, within Early Childhood Education (ECE) internationally there can be a broader understanding of that age range, from birth and in some cases up to eight. We believe that it is important to share a range of projects, and this is very much an early years project with its focus on Reception Class children and meeting their needs in developing speaking and listening skills. We also thought it would be helpful to include a specific intervention from a published and researched source. Although we would not advocate merely importing a particular programme/intervention based solely upon its purported value, this example action research project demonstrates how the use of prepared programmes can contribute to a broader investigation into an aspect of a provision.

Talking Partners was originally conceived in Bradford as a response to increasing numbers of children with English as an additional language (EAL). The Bradford Local Education Authority advisors from the Bradford Language and Literacy and Ethnic Minority Support team at the time designed and created the implementation which was rolled out with great success across Bradford and surrounding areas. As a result, it became well known and adopted across England and beyond. When the Local Authority Education system disbanded as a result of the end of the National Strategy in 2010, the intervention rebranded and continued as "Talking Partners@ Primary". The intervention is designed to be short-term, running for ten weeks for a group of children, although it can be used with individuals and whole classes. It aims to improve children's speaking and listening through a structured programme led by a trained adult. Children are selected based on an initial assessment, and the programme focuses on those who have EAL but have had some exposure, at least a year, to English rather than those completely new to it. The intervention collects data on its implementation and these are collated into reports available on their website. This is helpful in enabling practitioners to see whether it would be effective for their setting and meet their needs in an evidence informed manner.

https://www.educationworks.org.uk/what-we-do/speaking-and-listening/talkingpartnersprimary.

Project summary

This project implemented the Talking Partners intervention with six children identified as needing support with their speaking and listening development. The intervention lasts ten weeks and was led by a trained adult. It used an initial assessment and this is repeated at the end to show progress. This is a good example of an evidence informed project, whereby a tried and tested intervention with research and data has been explored as part of a school focus and mediated to meet the needs of the children and context. They decided upon the research question – How can the intervention "Talking Partners at Primary" enhance children's speaking and listening skills?

5. Considering the future

To run the intervention for the new reception intake, the school decided to undertake the following further activities for the project (Autumn):

To run the intervention in both Key Stage 1 and Key Stage 2.

To train additional staff to deliver "Talking Partners at Primary".

To assess the children using Language Link and the Renfrew Action Picture test.

4. Evaluating impact

After only four weeks of the intervention, all of the children were showing progress in:
Speaking and listening.
Speaking with confidence in groups and in whole class situations.
Sentence structure formation, including the children's use of grammar.
Including more detail in their everyday talk having an impact on their learning.
Using English confidently within the school in all contexts.

1. Identifying a focus

Previous analysis raised the issue of children with less well-developed oral language leading to a school focus and action plan. Observations including photos, video clips, children speaking, and Autumn 2 data demonstrated that although the children were showing more confidence, interacting with their peers, speaking more in class, and had made good progress, they were still below expectations. This was having an impact on other areas of their learning. As a school, we decided that we needed more than the quality first teaching that was being provided and the speaking and listening groups. As a school, we decided to introduce the intervention "Talking Partners at Primary" in the early years. Creating our research question: How can Talking Partners intervention enhance children's speaking and listening skills?

2. Collating information

Baseline Assessment and Language Link demonstrated that 35% of children were below the expected level in speaking and listening. All of the children below expectations have EAL and are summer born. Three of the children below expectations did not have any pre-school experience.

3. Planning and implementing a change

As a formal intervention, we adopted Talking partners and set it up in our schools. It was implemented as a ten week programme, with three children per group for five 20 minute sessions per week in EYFS. Consists of a warm up and an activity.

We decided that two of the children below expectation would not be part of the intervention as they were new to English and did not have enough English vocabulary to participate.

We identified six children and grouped them into two groups of three.

Five of the identified children were below expectations in speaking and listening. The sixth child was as expected in speaking and listening, but lacked confidence whilst speaking and often did not talk in sentences.

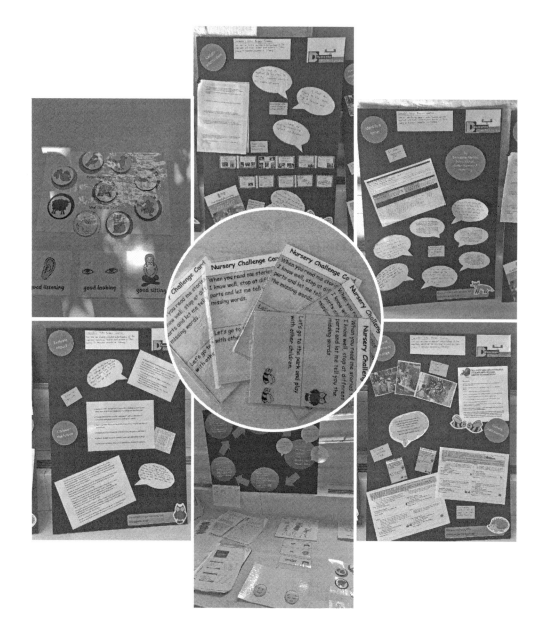

7 Parental engagement

Common sense and research combine to identify parental engagement in children's education as crucial for their success. The longitudinal research project Effective Provision in Pre-School Education (EPPE) which later expanded to cover primary and secondary education and came to be known as EPPSE, tracked over 3,000 children and their earliest education experiences throughout a seventeen year period. The study identified factors that impacted children's progress in a range of measures and the level of parental education, engagement, and communication with settings had a significant influence (Siraj-Blatchford et al., 2003).

There is a great deal of research on the importance for settings in engaging with parents to benefit children's outcomes (Fan & Williams, 2010) as well as literature outlining the challenges of "hard-to-reach" parents who find relationships with settings challenging for a variety of reasons (Goodall & Montgomery, 2014). As a result, settings work hard to involve parents and operate a range of initiatives to build positive relationships.

The action research project was undertaken by a team of EYFS teachers within a school-based setting, which included a two-year-old provision. This project started from a discussion between the EYFS teachers about ways to address apparent Early Years Foundation Stage Profile (EYFSP) data trends in children's literacy, and a sense of differing parental perceptions about the skills that children needed for school. During home visits, the teachers had become increasingly aware that parents, keen to support their children prepare for entry to school, were prioritising aspects of reading and writing that didn't specifically coincide with the approach to holistic development advocated by the setting. Through team discussion, they shared ideas about their focus and decided that they wanted to explore ways to promote the prime areas of learning to parents and engender an understanding of the milestones that contributed to children's development in literacy.

Project summary

This was a complex project combining working with parents, children, and colleagues to reconsider the messages that the school was sending about learning within the EYFS. Emerging from discussion between teachers, the EYFS team developed the research question – *"How can we develop parental understanding of the important milestones children must achieve in their journey to being successful in literacy"*. The process for developing, and investigating, this research question required continuous reflection and collaboration to consider and reconsider perceptions of school-based learning and differing expectations of children's development.

5. Considering the future

The setting had considered the timing of the introduction of the challenge cards and planned to develop the process further the following year. They also reflected upon the broader messages that some of their previous homework activities were sending to parents about the school's priorities, so they planned to redevelop their approach to homework throughout the EYFS to place greater emphasis upon the importance of the prime areas of learning from the outset of the new school year.

4. Evaluating impact

Following the initial introduction of the challenge cards, the short-term impact was considered by further discussions with parents and practitioner views on the children's engagement with the home learning activities. However, the teachers felt that the timing of the introduction of the cards, in June, had limited the impact of the cards, and the evaluation of the impact of them. Longer term goals were set for further developing the cards for introduction at the start of the new school year and sharing the intentions of the cards with parents from the point of entry.

The teachers also reflected upon the impact of the process for their own development, individually and as a team, and noted some important factors that the discussions had enabled them to question their own, and each other's, practice across the EYFS provision at the school.

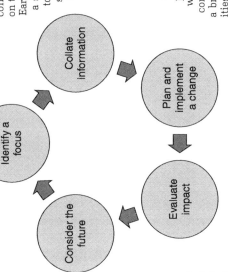

1. Identifying a focus

During the initial phase of the project, the teachers knew that they wanted to focus on literacy and explored what was already happening within the provision to consider what aspect of literacy needed to be the focus in order to contribute to improving data outcomes. The discussion led them to share experiences from home visits and contemplate their perception of parental expectations of children's literacy development in relation to the school's priorities and practices.

2. Collating information

Following their initial discussions, the teachers wanted to explore parental expectations further. They organised a coffee morning to speak to parents about their current views on the important aspects of children's progress towards the Early Learning Goals for reading and writing. They devised a short survey to investigate parents' views in detail and to gather ideas about the possible activities that the school could introduce to support parents further. The coffee morning included some informal conversations which, when discussed as a team, suggested that the school could do more to promote the importance of the prime areas of learning and their value in supporting children's development in all areas.

3. Planning and implementing a change

The EYFS teachers considered various approaches to prioritising the message that the prime areas of learning were key to supporting children's development, and considered their current homework practices. In line with a broader school initiative in developing homework activities, they decided to adapt the homework provided within the EYFS, to establish a more activity-based approach. The teachers developed "challenge cards" for home learning, which included simple tasks involving conversation, physical, and play activities for children and parents to complete together each week. The teachers created an information sheet to explain the introduction of the challenge cards and the value of the activities for supporting children's development through the variety of activities suggested.

8 Early writing

As adults, we often take for granted the ability to write and forget the complex processes we have learnt in order to be effective orchestrators of the many elements involved in both transcription and composition that are required for successful writing. Indeed, the fast-changing developments in technologies make some wonder if writing is a necessary skill. However, it remains a bedrock of the education curriculum and learning process, and its complexities create many levels and layers of skills, knowledge, and understanding that children need to learn to be successful. The simple task of writing a caption involves first having something to say, an idea, and then having the vocabulary and oral language to compose a grammatically correct utterance that can be orally rehearsed and identified as a suitable caption text in terms of audience and purpose. A good understanding of the written code of punctuation, alphabetical symbols including formation, and concepts about print (Clay, 2002) including spatial awareness, print layout, and left-to-right and top-to-bottom orientation in English is required. This is followed by the physical act of holding a pen in an appropriate grip, coordinating hand and eye to make a mark on paper with the correct pressure – too much and the paper tears or the writing implement breaks, too little and the marks are not seen. Posture is important to prevent muscle strain, and the height and arrangement of furniture and equipment affect the physical ability to write. Memory plays a part too; the message must be retained and remembered in sequence and the progress of capturing that message, and checking on the progress, perhaps by re-reading, occurs. This long description provides a small insight into the complex cognitive and physical learning that each child requires to participate in a writing activity. This helps to explain why so many children find aspects of writing hard and why so many practitioners want to support children's development and learning in this area. It also clarifies how easy it is to start with one idea about what aspect of the whole process might support children's development. And it reinforces the need to think carefully, reflect on the initial focus, and collate data in case there is another factor that might require focussed consideration as it will have a greater influence on children's outcomes.

In creating this book, we had several projects that practitioners shared with us that focussed on different aspects of early writing. After some debate, we chose this one, not because the others were less successful, but because this project highlights the cyclical nature of action research. Sometimes, practitioners might think that the process is linear – from identifying the focus to carrying out the project everything progresses in a straight line, as it were, through the different stages. The reality we want to share is that constant reflection is required and the cycles support practitioners in evaluating throughout and potentially changing direction, or starting a new cycle in light of their reflections, data, and children's needs. The project that follows exemplifies this change of direction.

Project summary

This project was a collaboration between the lead for English and the Early Years lead in an infant school. It began with a shared interest in early writing and supporting children to make progress. Practitioners were also aware of children's experiences of transition from nursery to reception and then into year 1 and the changing expectations and pedagogies around early writing. The project began with a question about how to develop children's oral language through storytelling as way to support early writing. However, the collaborative approach taken by lead practitioners quickly meant that the project evolved and the question became one about the physical processes required for early writing.

5. Considering the future

The introduction of the simple "draw an x" assessment for handwriting readiness has made a huge difference, and this is now consistently used throughout the Early Years Foundation Stage (EYFS). We plan to embed this approach and the consistency of the implementation so that it becomes part of our routine and not just the project.

4. Evaluating impact

Children have a greater understanding about how their letters need to be formed. The activities and assessment mean that practitioners can easily see whether to challenge or support a child and the children can make progress within the lesson. Observations show that the children are engaged and excited about writing. Children are more confident and motivated to write independently. They take great pride in their writing and want to show it to adults. The observations and examples of children's work show progress with sample of before and after illustrating a change greater than the passage of time development expected. We anticipate the Foundation Stage Profile data and the transition documentation will offer evidence of impact.

Identify a focus → Collate information → Plan and implement a change → Evaluate impact → Consider the future →

1. Identifying a focus

The project began with a focus on oral language and storytelling, and we attended helicopter storytelling training, which was amazing. But when we began to delve deeper, we realised the issue for our children was about the physical barriers to writing rather than oral language. It became a transcriptional rather than compositional issue. Children were reluctant writers because of the physical barriers, not because they lacked motivation or something to say. So, we went down the gross motor, fine motor, and handwriting route because from observations this was a bigger barrier. This led us to shift again from "how can we engage reluctant writers?" to considering "how does children's handwriting develop?" and "how can this positively impact the writing process?"

2. Collating information

We found that the children were natural storytellers, particularly this cohort, so we didn't need to work on oral language. We did some research; there was so much on handwriting, but the main points were that we needed to see if the children were ready for formal handwriting and not force them into it too quickly.

3. Planning and implementing a change

Together we formulated a plan which was informed by the reading and research we did and implemented across the classes. Research provided an assessment for readiness for formal handwriting teaching. If the children could draw an x, they were ready. This meant we could assess children daily and move them on as appropriate. Handwriting was taught and modelled daily. Handwriting was differentiated for individual children. Fine motor activities were made available. Letter families were displayed in every classroom and misconceptions about letter formation picked up very quickly and addressed. There was consistency across all the classes.

9 Promoting a love of reading

In international comparisons of countries' educational performance using the Progress in International Reading Literacy Study (PIRLS), England appears in the top half on the international rankings, but it also has a very long tail of under-achievement, suggesting that whilst we have high-attaining results, we have also consistently failed to close the achievement gap despite large-scale policy initiatives (Beard, 2000). This tail of underachievement in reading is not only in decoding and comprehension but also in enjoyment and choosing to read for pleasure, and it has been the focus for a number of years.

Ofsted's report "Reading for Pleasure" (2012) highlights the issues and calls for action. Since then, the discussion about how to teach reading has shifted from the "reading wars" approach of the place of phonics and the balance within the simple view of reading between decoding and comprehension (Smith, 2018) and into the importance of children reading to learn and to enjoy books and all forms of reading material. This shift echoes the work of many practitioners who are passionate about reading and helping children to be successful and motivated readers.

The following project highlights the work of a nursery in engaging parents, children, and practitioners in a range of reading activities designed to support a life-long love of reading. It is interesting in that it draws upon a range of external opportunities and findings that offered opportunities to create a larger-scale project than might have been possible using existing nursery resources.

Project summary

This project is a multifaceted approach taken by one nursery to develop a holistic approach to promoting a love of reading in children and their families, with the nursery at the heart of the initiatives. They were able to access external funding and opportunities from charities to support their work, and this is something that other settings might consider too. Involving parents and the local community can be a powerful resource for any setting, but it can also take additional time and effort to communicate the aims and objectives of any project and then to recruit, train, and retain volunteers.

5. Considering the future

The project was complex as there were three strands to it which involved external agencies and the community as well as the setting. So, for the future it will be key to maintain the momentum and build capacity so that when families move on and leave, there are still enough volunteers and enthusiasm to maintain the initiatives. Regular updating of the learning environment to keep the children's engagement is a core action.

4. Evaluating impact

This project collected quantitative and qualitative data to assess and evaluate the progress of the project. Audits of children's book area usage were taken before and after the changes, photos of book areas captured the changes made, counts were made of the actual number of children choosing to read not just in the book areas but across the provision, and children, staff, and parental perceptions were collected and compared. Data showed a shift from a third to half the children independently engaging in books for enjoyment in a three-month period.

1. Identifying a focus

The nursery is part of a teaching school alliance and they chose the focus in light of data, nursery development priorities, and the opportunity to be part of charitable initiatives focussed on developing reading for pleasure.

2. Collating information

Photos, audits, and observations created a record of current practice. Research identified opportunities from Beanstalk and other charities as well as resources such as the website www.lovemybooks.co.uk which is an evidence-informed site supporting parents and practitioners with ideas and resources for promoting a love of reading.

3. Planning and implementing a change

The project took a three-strand approach utilising national and charitable organisation initiatives to develop reading for pleasure. The nursery introduced an "Anytime is story time bear" which was sent home with children with a storybook and notebook helping to engage parents with the project. The setting developed its reading areas with more resources including puppets and costumes for storytelling and bigger spaces with more comfort. The nursery also signed up for the Beanstalk charity and Dolly Parton "Story Starter" initiative funded by the Postcode Lottery which provides books for children from disadvantaged areas. Parents and volunteers were recruited and trained to read with children twice a week for 20 minutes.

Identify a focus → Collate information → Plan and implement a change → Evaluate impact → Consider the future

10 0–2-year-old room

This project initially started from an Early Years Educator's (EYE) desire to explore motivations for a specific practice, with a view to developing it from a position of understanding. The action research process caused the educator to also consider her own approach to leading practice through collaboration and discussion, as it exposed some additional factors in the team's differing beliefs in their roles for contributing to decision-making.

In addition to institutional structures for formal leadership and management responsibilities, Early Years Foundation Stage (EYFS) settings can often have models of pedagogical leadership which are distributed amongst practitioners at different levels of qualification and experience. This, however, can lead to assumptions about roles and responsibilities if notions of pedagogical leadership and practitioner responsibility for leading practice are not embedded within a broader ethos (Siraj-Blatchford and Hallet, 2013; Male and Nicholson, 2016). The shift in emphasis from conceptions of leadership in leading people to collective responsibilities for leadership of practice became an inadvertent focus of this setting's action research and intentions for future development in response to the action research project. This project illustrates the importance of pedagogical leadership and its dependence upon broader organisational structures and ethos (Male and Nicholson, 2016).

Project summary

This project was initially started by a new EYE joining a setting, who noticed that some aspects of practice were more structured by practical considerations within the setting than pedagogical motivations. As a new member of staff, the EYE was interested in aspects of practice that established practitioners accepted as "the way things are done". As such, a fresh view of practice led to the development of systems within the setting and a continued professional dialogue influenced by multiple voices.

5. Considering the future

During the action research process, the EYE became aware that some practitioners had ideas about practice within the setting which they were not confident to express or did not feel suitably senior enough to make suggestions about. Developing systems for obtaining, and valuing, perspectives from all practitioners became a focus for further investigation within the setting.

The system developed for planning learning activities and sharing responsibilities at carpet time was also shared between partner settings.

4. Evaluating impact

Following the development of carpet time to include resources and planned learning opportunities, the EYE completed a further observation of children's participation. She noted significant reduction in children being overtly reluctant to participate and an increase in practitioners attempting to engage children in group activity, rather than "contain" them. In addition, the EYE was able to establish a process for ensuring that all practitioners could input into the further development of carpet time and suggestions for activities. This, in turn, resulted in collaborative reflection upon processes for developing other aspects of the setting's routine.

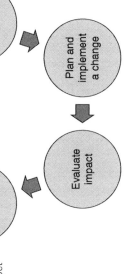

1. Identifying a focus

The initial focus was determined by a desire to understand aspects of the setting's routine more fully. The EYE had noticed that all children were required to participate in a group "carpet time" just before lunch, but the pedagogical utility of this was unclear as many children appeared reluctant to participate and many practitioners appeared uncertain of their role in activities.

2. Collating Information

The EYE observed practice, recording observations of the children's actions during the transition to carpet time. She then spoke to practitioners and devised a questionnaire to find out about individual perspectives on the role of carpet time with 0- to 2-year-old children and the reason for establishing this as part of the setting's routine. This identified that many practitioners viewed carpet time as a necessity in order to allow the room to be safely set up for lunchtime. The safety practicalities of having all of the children involved in a group activity were primarily seen as the motivation for the practice, and this notion of "containment" directed practitioner activity during carpet time. Through the process of collecting information, the EYE also found out that several practitioners had ideas for how this aspect of the routine could be developed differently, but they had not been confident to question or adapt it.

3. Planning and implementing a change

By interrogating all practitioners' perspectives on the development of "carpet time" within the provision, the EYE was able to devise a system, in collaboration with all practitioners, for planning varied and engaging learning activities that attempted to motivate group participation. In recognising the importance of the practical motivation for group carpet time at a particular point in the day, the EYE was able to also develop an emphasis upon the learning opportunities that could be created at this time and clarify expectations of all practitioners.

Conclusion

These projects reflect a range of foci, all identified by practitioners as both personally and professionally interesting and relevant to the individual settings and contexts. They showcase a small number of projects from the many that early years practitioners are engaged with, but which, we hope, provide an overview of the range, diversity, and interests of the amazing practitioners that care for and educate our children. The projects also reflect the differing types of engagement and comfort with action research as a methodology. For some settings there were challenges with accessing and reading journal articles to develop subject knowledge, or to gain ideas for change, or how to assess impact; for others it was discussing types of data such as qualitative and quantitative measures. But throughout, the commitment and passion of all in wanting to make a difference to the outcomes of children drove the projects. From a pure research perspective such as the "what works" positivist perspective promoted and exemplified through randomised control studies, some outcomes may be seen as less robust or scientific. But much research within education is qualitative, small-scale, and interpretivist, enabling researchers and practitioners to understand in detail the rich interactions that characterise the complex world of early years. Action research does that and so much more, it allows practitioners to be the "agents of change" that characterise professionals and leaders whose work is underpinned by "moral purpose" in the service of children and their families.

We hope that these examples of action research projects, in addition to the discussions and explanations within the text as a whole, have contributed to an understanding of both the power and applicability of action research within the EYFS. As pedagogical leaders, all practitioners have a role in shaping practice and a responsibility towards the development of the provision. It is hoped that through exemplification of how action research can contribute to this within EYFS settings, practitioners at all levels will consider its value for the development of individuals, teams, environments, and children.

References

Adelman, C. (1993) 'Kurt Lewin and the Origins of Action Research', *Educational Action Research*, 1(1), pp. 7–24.

Beard, R. (2000) 'Research and the National Literacy Strategy', *Oxford Review of Education*, 26(3), pp. 421–436.

BERA. (2018b) *Ethical Guidelines for Educational Research*, 4th ed. London, British Educational Research Association.

Bertram, T., Formosinho, J., Gray, C., Pascal, C. and Whalley, M. (2015) Ethical Code for Early Childhood Researchers. EECERA (EECERA 2015 Ethical code for early childhood researchers). http://eecera-ext.tandf.co.uk/documents/pdf/organisation/EECERA-Ethical-Code.pdf.

Biesta, G. J. J. (2010) 'Why "What Works" Still Won't Work: From Evidence-Based Education to Value-Based Education', *Studies in Philosophy and Education*, 29(5), pp. 491–503.

Bradbury, A. and Roberts-Holmes, G. (2017) *The Datafication of Primary and Early Years Education*, Oxon, Routledge.

Brown, C. and Rogers, S. (2015) 'Measuring the Effectiveness of Knowledge Creation as a Means of Facilitating Evidence-Informed Practice in Early Years Settings in One London Borough', *London Review of Education*, 12(3), pp. 245–260.

Bryce-Clegg, A. (2013) *Getting Ready to Write*, London, Featherstone Education.

Bubb, S. and Earley, P. (2007) *Leading and Managing Continuing Professional Development*, 2nd ed., London, Paul Chapman Publishing.

Carr, W. and Kemmis, S. (1986) *Becoming Critical: Education, Knowledge, and Action Research*, Abingdon, Falmer Press.

Clark, A. (2005) 'Ways of Seeing: Using the Mosaic Approach to Listen to Children's Perspectives'. In Clark, A. and Kjorholt, A. T., and Moss, P. (eds) *Beyond listening to Children's perspectives on early childhood*, Bristol, Policy Press, pp. 29–49.

Clay, M. (2002) *An Observation Survey of Early Literacy Achievement*, 2nd ed., Portsmouth NH, Heinemann.

Clay, M., Gill, M., Glynn, T., McNaughton, T. and Salmon, K. (1983) *Record of Oral Language and Biks and Gutches*, Auckland, Pearson Education New Zealand.

Coldwell, M. and Simkins, T. (2011) 'Level Models of Continuing Professional Development Evaluation: A Grounded Review and Critique', *Professional Development in Education*, 37, pp. 143–157.

Corey, S. (1954) "Action Research in Education", *The Journal of Educational Research*, 47(5), pp. 375–380.

Cremin, T., Flewitt, R., Mardell, B. and Swann, J., eds. (2017) *Storytelling in Early Childhood: Enriching Language, Literacy and Classroom Culture*, London, Routledge.

Diamond, A. and Lee, K. (2011) 'Interventions Shown to Aid Executive Function Development in Children 4–12 Years Old', *Science*, 333(6045), pp. 959–964. DOI: 10.1126/science.1204529

Dickens, L. and Watkins, K. (2006) 'Action Research: Rethinking Lewin', In Gallos, J. (ed.), *Organization Development*, San Francisco, Jossey-Bass.

Earley, P. and Porritt, V., eds. (2009) *Effective Practices in Continuing Professional Development: Lessons from Schools*, London, IOE.

Earley, P. and Porritt, V., eds. (2010) *Effective Practices in Continuing Professional Development Lessons from Schools*, London, Institute of Education Press.

Earley, P. and Porritt, V. (2013) 'Evaluating the Impact of Professional Development: The Need for a Student-Focused Approach', *Professional Development in Education*, 40(1), pp. 112–129.

Elliott, J. (1991) *Action Research for Educational Change*, Buckingham, Open University Press.

Elliott, J. (2007) 'Making Evidence-Based Practice Educational', In Hammersley, M. (ed.), *Educational Research and Evidence-Based Practice*, London, SAGE. pp. 66–88.

European Union. (2013) *The Attractiveness of the Teaching Profession in Europe*, Luxembourg, European Union.

Fan, W. and Williams, C. M. (2010) 'The Effects of Parental Involvement on Students' Academic Self-Efficacy, Engagement and Intrinsic Motivation', *Educational Psychology: An International Journal of Experimental Educational Psychology*, 30(1), pp. 53–74.

Fullan, M. and Ballew, A. (2004) *Leading in a Culture of Change Personal Action Guide and Workbook*, San Francisco, Jossey-Bass.

General Teaching Council for England. (2006) *What Is Research-Engaged Professional Practice ? How Does This Help the School, the Teacher and the Learner?* London, General Teaching Council for England.

Goodall, J. and Montgomery, C. (2014) 'Parental Involvement to Parental Engagement: A Continuum', *Educational Review*, 66(4), pp. 399–410.

Guskey, T. (2000) *Evaluating Professional Development*, London, SAGE Publications Ltd.

Hammersley, M. (2007) 'Educational Research and Teaching: A Response to David Hargreaves' TTA Lecture', In Hammersley, M. (ed.), *Educational Research and Evidence-Based Practice*, London, SAGE Publications Ltd., pp. 18–42.

Handscombe, G. and McBeath, J. (2003) *The Research Engaged School*, Chelmsford, UK, Essex Forum for Learning and Research Enquiry (FLARE), pp. 1–16.

Hargreaves, D. H. (1996). *Teaching as a Research Based Profession: Possibilities and Prospects*, London, Teacher Training Agency.

Hargreaves, D. H. (1999) 'Revitalising Educational Research: Lessons from the Past and Proposals for the Future Revitalising Educational Research: Lessons from the Past and Proposals for the Future', *Cambridge Journal of Education*, 29(2), pp. 239–249.

Hargreaves, D. H. (2007a) 'In Defence of Research for Evidence-Based Teaching: A Rejoinder to Martyn Hammersley', In Hammersley, M. (ed.), *Educational Research and Evidence-based Practice*, London, SAGE, pp. 43–60.

Hargreaves, D. H. (2007b) 'Teaching as a Research-Based Profession: Possibilities and Prospects', In Hammersley, M. (ed.), *Educational Research and Evidence-Based Practice*, London, SAGE, pp. 3–17.

Kemmis, S. (2007) 'Action Research', In Hammersley, M. (ed.), *Educational Research and Evidence-Based Practice*, London, SAGE, pp. 167–180.

Kirkpatrick, D. L. (1959) 'Techniques for Evaluation Training Programs', *Journal of the American Society of Training Directors*, 13, pp. 21–26.

Lewin, K. (1946) 'Action Research and Minority Problems', *Journal of Social Issues*, 2(4), pp. 34–46.

Macklem, G. L. (2008) *Practitioner's Guide to Emotion Regulation in School Aged Children*, Boston, MA, Springer US. DOI:10.1007/978-0-387-73851-2

Male, T. (2012). 'Ethical Leadership in Early Years Settings', In Palaiologou, I. (ed.), *Ethical Practice in Early Childhood*, London, SAGE.

Male, T. and Nicholson, N. (2016) 'Leadership in Early Years Foundation Stage', In Palaiologou, I. (ed.), *The Early Years Foundation Stage Theory and Practice*, 3rd ed, London, SAGE.

Manion and Cohen. (1994) *Research Methods in Education*, London, Routledge.

Masters, J. (1995) 'The History of Action Research', In Hughs, I. (ed.), *Action Research Electronic Reader*, Camperdown, NSW, The University of Sydney (Online).

McAteer, M. (2014) 'What Is This Thing Called Action Research?', In *Action Research in Education*, London, SAGE, pp. 1–14.

McNiff, J. (2002) *Action Research for Professional Development Concise Advice for New Action Researchers*, 3rd ed. www.jeanmcniff.com.

McNiff, J. (2013) *Action Research: Principles and Practice*, 3rd ed, Abingdon, Taylor & Francis.

McNiff, J. (2015) *Writing Up Your Action Research Project*, Abingdon, Routledge.

Norbury, C., Gooch, D., Baird, G., Charman, T., Simonoff, E. and Pickles, A. (2016) 'Younger Children Experience Lower Levels of Language Competence and Academic Progress in the First Year of School: Evidence from a Population Study', *Journal of Child Psychology and Psychiatry*, 57(1), pp. 65–73.

Nutbrown, C. (2012) *Foundations for Quality the Independent Review of Early Education and Childcare Qualifications*, Cheshire, Department for Education.

Palaiologou, I. (2012) *Ethical Practice in Early Childhood*, London, SAGE.

Peters, M. and Robinson, V. (1984) 'The Origin and Status of Action Research', *The Journal of Applied Behavioral Science*, 20(2), pp. 113–124.

Porritt, V. (2013) 'Evaluating the Impact of Professional Learning', In Crowley, S. (ed.), *Challenging Professional Learning*, Abingdon, Taylor & Francis, pp. 77–100.

Powell, B. (2012) 'Ethics, Policy and Every Child Matters', In Palaiologou, I. (ed.), *Ethical Practice in Early Childhood*, London, SAGE.

Razza, R. A., Bergen-Cico, D. and Raymond, K. (2013). 'Enhancing Pre-Schoolers' Self-Regulation via Mindful Yoga', *Journal of Child and Family Studies*, 24(2), pp. 372–385. DOI: 10.1007/s10826-013-9847-6.

Roberts-Holmes, G. (2018) *Doing Your Early Rears Research Project*, 4th ed, London, SAGE.

Robson, C. (2011) *Real World Research*, 3rd ed, Chichester, Wiley.

Siraj-Blatchford, I. (2009). 'Conceptualising Progression in the Pedagogy of Play and Sustained Shared Thinking in Early Childhood Education: A Vygotskian Perspective'. *Education and Child Psychology*, 26(2), pp. 77–89.

Siraj-Blatchford, I. and Hallet, E. (2013) *Effective and Caring Leadership in Early Years*, London, Sage.

Siraj-Blatchford, I. and Manni, L. (2007), *Effective Leadership in the Early Years Sector: The ELEYS Study*, London, IOE Press.

Siraj-Blatchford, I., Sylva, K., Taggart, B., Sammons, P., Melhuish, E. and Elliot, K. (2003) *The Effective Provision of Pre-School Education (EPPE) Project Intensive Case Studies of Practice across the Foundation: The Effective Provision of Pre-School*, London, IOE Press.

Smith, J. E. (2018) 'Re-Engineering National Reading Policy, Pedagogy, and Professional Development: The Case for a Simple View of Meaningful Reading', *TEAN Journal*, 10(2), pp. 65–79.

Somekh, B. (1995) 'The Contribution of Action Research to Development in Social Endeavours: A Position Paper on Action Research Methodology', *British Educational Research Journal*, 21(35), pp. 339–355.

Somekh, B. (2010) 'The Collaborative Action Research Network: 30 Years of Agency in Developing Educational Action Research', *Educational Action Research*, 18(1), pp. 103–121.

Spencer, T., Dietrich, R. and Slocum, T. (2012) 'Evidence-Based Practice: A Framework for Making Effective Decisions', *Education and Treatment of Children*, 35(2), pp. 127–151. DOI: 10.1353/etc.2012.0013.

Stenhouse, L. (1981) 'What Counts as Research?', *British Journal of Educational Studies*, 29(2), pp. 103–114.

Stoll, L., Harris, A. and Handscomb, G. (2012) *Great Professional Development which Leads to Great Pedagogy: Nine Claims from Research*, Nottingham, National College for School Leadership.

Timperley, H. and Earl, L. M. (2008) 'Using Conversations to Make Sense of Evidence: Possibilities and Pitfalls', In Timperley, H. and Earl, L. M. (eds.), *Professional Learning Conversations: Challenges in Using Evidence for Improvement*, Berlin, Springer Science & Business, pp. 121–126.

Whorrall, J. and Cabell, S. (2016) 'Supporting Children's Oral Language Development in the Preschool Classroom', *Early Childhood Education Journal*, 44(4), pp. 335–341.

Winch, C., Oancea, A., Orchard. J. (2015) The Contribution of Educational Research to Teachers' Professional Learning: Philosophical Understandings, *Oxford Review of Education*, 41(2), pp. 202–216.

Winstanley, C. (2012) 'Alluring Ideas: Cherry-Picking Policy from Around the World', *Journal of Philosophy of Education*, 46(4), pp. 516–531.

World Health Organisation. (2003) *Creating an Environment for Emotional and Social Well-Being: An Important Responsibility of a Health Promoting and Child-friendly School*, Geneva, WHO.

Wyse, D., Brown, C., Oliver, S., and Poblete, X. (2018) 'The BERA "Close to Practice"', In Wyse, D. (ed.), *Research Intelligence*, London, British Educational Research Association, pp. 15–16.

Appendices

Appendix I: Identifying a focus

Collecting some initial thoughts

What are the biggest challenges within my/our practice or within the provision at the moment?

What influences/causes these challenges?

How much control do I/we have over the causes of these challenges?

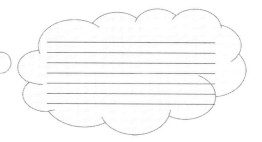

The most pressing aspect of practice/provision requiring closer scrutiny and adaptation is...

Appendix II: Collating evidence

What is the current situation in your chosen area of focus, and what evidence do you have to inform your view? What do you need to confirm/explore your view further?

What evidence/data do you already have?	What evidence/data do you still need?
Children ...?	Children ...?
You/your practice ...?	You/your practice ...?
Teachers/practitioners ...?	Teachers/practitioners ...?
Others ...?	Others ...?

What additional evidence/data might you need?
How and where will you get this?

Appendix III: Planning for impact

Focus of enquiry/research question _____

Baseline	Changes to be implemented	Impact
What are children achieving/ feeling/doing/saying now?		What will children be achieving/ feeling/doing/saying?
Children are ...		**Children will ...**
What is your practice like now?		What will your practice be like?
I am/we are ...		**I/we will...**

Source: Earley, P. and Porritt, V., eds. (2009) *Effective Practices in Continuing Professional Development: Lessons from Schools*, London, IOE.

Earley, P. and Porritt, V. (2013) 'Evaluating the Impact of Professional Development: The Need for a Student-Focused Approach', *Professional Development in Education*, 40(1), pp. 112–129.

The authors and publisher are grateful for permission to reproduce the following materials in this book from the London Centre for Leadership in Learning (LCLL) at UCL Institute of Education.

Appendix IV: Planning for impact

My research focus is ....

....

The current situation is ....

....

I know this because ....

....

The difference I want to make is ....

....

It will look like ....

....

The people it will involve are ....

....

The changes that I will introduce are ....

....

The data I will collect are ....

....

My action research cycle duration is ....

....

I need ....

Amanda Ince and Eleanor Kitto (2020), *A Practical Guide to Action Research and Teacher Enquiry*, Routledge

Appendix V: Evaluating impact

The process so far …

Use this pro forma to reflect upon the action research process to date and consider where you started, what you have done, and what difference this has made.

The research focus was ....

....

The initial situation was ....·

....

The evidence of this was ....

....

The change(s) that were implemented was/were ....

....

We envisioned that this would/might ....

....

The situation now is ....

The evidence of this is ....

Appendix VI: Considering the future

Summary and intentions
Use this pro forma to summarise what you have learned from the process so far, and consider where this might take you next.

Through the action research process I have learned ....

....

The biggest influence upon my professional learning has been ....

....

The biggest influence upon the team has been ....

....

The biggest influence upon the environment/provision/children has been ....

....

The biggest question that I am left with is ....

I may investigate this further by ....

Index

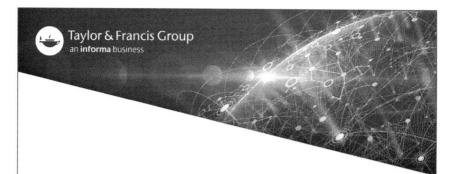